D0903821

Documentation and the Organization of Knowledge

Documentation and the Organization of Knowledge

By JESSE H. SHERA,
Dean of the School of Library Science,
Western Reserve University

Edited and with an Introduction
By D. J. FOSKETT, M.A., F.L.A.
Librarian, University of London Institute of Education

ARCHON BOOKS
HAMDEN, CONNECTICUT · 1966

PRINTED IN GREAT BRITAIN

Editor's Note

AS IN the previous volume of Dean Shera's essays, I have made a few modifications to the original texts where this seemed appropriate. By agreement with Dean Shera, I have not attempted to change passages that are now out-of-date, but have added more recent information in footnotes where these seemed necessary. In those essays and papers published originally in journals in the U.S.A. American spelling has been retained.

D.J.F.

Author's Note

In one sense the present volume may be regarded as a kind of tract, for the essays of which it is composed argue, from a variety of dimensions, the essential unity of librarianship. Ever since the author first read of the work of Otlet and La Fontaine and the Bruxelles Institute, and this has now been more years than he likes to recall, he has been convinced that there is more to the intellectual content of librarianship than was dreamed of by Melvil Dewey. This holistic view of the library world, then, has been a kind of *leitmotif* to accompany each of these collected entries into print.

In a second sense this collection of essays is our modest tribute to the pioneering work of S. C. Bradford, whose volume *Documentation*, which first appeared in 1948 still stands as a landmark. Bradford was certainly the father of documentation in the English-speaking world, and that his book now has little more than historical significance testifies to the rapidity with which the field is advancing, and in no way detracts from the importance of the contribution he made and the heritage he left behind. The original plan for the present volume was that it should 'bring *Bradford* up to date', but it soon became apparent that any attempt to revise his writings would distort his concept of what documentation is and do violence to his position in the library world. Therefore, the decision was made to leave Bradford's work untouched and devote these pages to a philosophy of documentation and librarianship for which we alone must assume responsibility, though the debt to Bradford remains great.

As we write these words, we have just returned from the Mid-Winter meetings of the American Library Association at which time the Council, which is the governing body of that organization, voted to establish within the ALA a Division of Automation and Information Science. We dare to hope that our thesis is winning support, not because we espoused it , but because it is so very right. 'These are tides running,' as we said in the essay of this volume on INTREX, 'and currents moving beneath the surface, that can dramatically reshape the coastline of librarianship,' and we might add, give librarianship a new continental identity. Perhaps this book may be a bit of flotsam, the drift of which may give the mariners of our profession some indication of the crests and troughs in what is, for the moment at least, a very restless sea.

So we say with Chaucer:

> Go, litel book . . .
> And kis the steppes, wher-as thou seest pace

not of 'Virgile, Ovyde, Omer, Lucan, and Stace.' but of Otlet, La Fontaine, and especially Bradford, and John Cotton Dana.

> And for ther is so greet diversitee
> In English and in wryting of our tongue,
> So preye I god that noon miswryte thee,
> Ne thee mismetre for defaute of tonge.
> And red wher-so thou be, or elles songe,
> That thou be understonde I god beseche!

February, 1966   J. H. SHERA

Contents

Editor's Note   v
Author's Note   vii
Introduction   xi

1 Documentation: Its Scope and Limitations   1
2 A Review of the Present State of Librarianship and
   Documentation   21
3 The Propaedentic of the New Librarianship   54
4 On Keeping Up with Keeping Up   72
5 Automation Without Fear   84
6 Developments in Machine Literature Searching   97
7 New Tools for Easing the Burden of Historical
   Research   108
8 Librarians' Pugwash, or *Intrex* on the Cape   115
9 Effect of Machine Methods on the Organization of
   Knowledge   123
10 Common Languages in Librarianship and Documentation   134
11 How Engineers Can Keep Abreast of Professional and
   Technical Developments   147
12 Automation and the Reference Librarian   158
13 The Recruiting of Technical Information Personnel   169
14 The Library as an Agency of Social Communication   174

   Index   179

Introduction

IN THE first volume of his collected essays, *Libraries and the Organization of Knowledge*, Dean J. H. Shera set out to explore the social foundations of modern librarianship, and their influence on the basic techniques of classification and cataloguing, together with the repercussions of these on the education of librarians. In this second series he discusses the refinements of those techniques, the newer techniques made possible by the introduction of computers, and the ways in which they help to make out the new rôle of this ancient profession: the rôle of documentation.

Although, as Shera continually emphasizes, documentation develops from librarianship, it has some aspects that are qualitatively new, and these have caused some specialists to draw a distinction between the two professions. Part of the purpose of this volume is to argue that there is no such distinction, that however much the branches of the activity may spread and ramify, the parent tree is the same. The early pioneers of modern librarianship (not forgetting Edward Edwards) looked to librarianship to keep pace with developing social needs and with industrial technology, and even though it cannot perhaps be claimed that subsequent efforts have been entirely successful, great advances have indeed been made.

It is not easy to find out precisely where the failure originated, but there may be some significance in the fact that the great era of development in the basic techniques of bibliography, cataloguing, and classification, occurred in the half-century from 1870, and that the refinement of these techniques took place in large general libraries, at the very moment when the accumulation of knowledge was beginning to force scholars themselves into specialization. In the general library one finds difficulties in identifying readers' objectives, and in becoming continuously associated with readers' pursuit of their objectives; thus the outstanding expressions of librarians' philosophies in the nineteenth century tended to concern themselves with general social aims – eliminating illiteracy, raising moral standards, giving access to 'good literature', and so forth. These are certainly worth pursuing, but we can hardly claim that they acted as an irresistible force, least of all in the late nineteenth century, in the way that industrial research has acted on libraries in the twentieth.

This lack of positive identification with readers' objectives had its valuable aspect, of course, for it obliged librarians to formulate their philosophies in terms of these larger aims; in terms, that is, of society as a whole, and not of any particular group. In the universities, this marched well with the notion of the pursuit of learning for its own sake, as opposed to vocational training. I should not wish to underestimate the value of this approach, because I think that it is due for a revival, and that professional librarianship will be subjected to another searching scrutiny in the light of social needs. Now, however, a new and important factor will be present – the experience derived from librarianship in special libraries and information services.

For what chiefly characterized the older form of librarianship was its preoccupation with the building of a collection, that is, with the problems of acquisition and management. How often have we heard the complaint that the road to the top of the profession lay through the administrative departments, and not through bibliography and reference service, which are, nevertheless, the core of professional activity! Of the three main phases – acquisition, arrangement, use – it was the first two that attracted most attention. The study of sources, book selection and identification, classification and cataloguing, and, above all, the administration of buildings and staff, these were the techniques in which professional librarians received training; and since it was the last which often required the most portentous decisions, chief librarians tended to be chosen for their administrative abilities rather than their skill in reference service, which hardly ever impressed itself upon governing bodies. In the literature, the administrative aspects came to predominate, and still do. Even the Aslib *Handbook of Special Librarianship*, and Irene Strieby and Lucille J. Strauss' *Scientific and Technical Libraries: their organization and administration* devote more space to these than to the use of library stocks.

But it was in the special library that the need for active dissemination of information existed, because the special library is set up for the specific purpose of providing information, usually within a limited range of subjects, to a known group of users who are pursuing certain readily identifiable objectives. The emphasis therefore falls upon the supply of information, and not upon the methods used to obtain it, important though these are. In what is probably the best introduction to this phase, the chapter on 'Reference and information work' in the Aslib *Handbook*, C. W. Hanson has analysed the basic reference situation and shown both how hard it is to reduce it to an orderly process, and yet how necessary it is if one is to achieve the desired ends quickly and efficiently.

To put it in the simplest form: the basic need of special library users is for 'bits' of information; Hanson's chapter includes a description of the various ways in which a request may be put, and he stresses first of all the need for a general scheme of concepts into which a request may be fitted. Without such a scheme, 'the searcher is left without any understanding of what he has found and can only pass the information on as blindly as he found it'. This underlines the theme that runs through all of Shera's essays: it is true that the nature of the information sought in libraries has changed, but the basic techniques have not changed. They certainly need to be improved and refined, but the need for them remains.

In the traditional form of library service, readers were usually expected to know the author or title of the document they wanted; in other words, they were expected to have done their own bibliographical searching before they came to the library. But an author/title inquiry still requires some searching, to find whether the library has the document and where it is filed. It is still necessary to transform the reader's statement into a catalogue entry which gives this extra piece of information. Subject inquiries are no different, in practice. The basic function of the librarian is to express the reader's need in words that can be found in a subject catalogue or bibliography – an entry that tells where the information is filed. What is radically new is the narrowing down of subject inquiries to 'bits' of information, and the corresponding increase in the precision sought from subject indexes.

Traditional librarianship has often been criticized for failing to deal with the 'subject approach', but it is not true to say that it was ignored. In the U.S.A., the Library of Congress and the universities set a good example with subject cataloguing, and the many series of indexes to periodicals testify to a real awareness of guides based on subject entries, as well as author. In the United Kingdom it was the public libraries that led the way, but since 1950 the *British National Bibliography* has provided a subject catalogue of new books, deposited under the Copyright Act, which has made an inestimable contribution to reference service. In the 1930s the names of Jennie Flexner, of the New York Public Library, and Herbert Woodbine, of Birmingham City Library, come to mind as outstanding exponents of information service in general libraries. Woodbine once wrote that service in a reference library tends to become research into subjects, instead of merely finding books that have been asked for by name.

So the elements already existed of the activities that formed the growth points in new directions under the impact of the great increase in specialist literature and the more demanding readership that came with it. The services growing out of these elements have two bases, variously named, which cater for the two outstanding needs of specialists and research workers: a current awareness service, and retrospective literature searching. Together these make up the field covered by Shera in this book: the field of documentation.

Consider first the retrospective search, because this must clearly be based on techniques already familiar to librarians – the accurate and detailed recording of all that comes into the library, and a close acquaintance with the bibliographical tools of the trade. What influence has the arrival of documentation had on these? It is mainly in the realm of subject indexing, for author cataloguing had already been brought to a high standard of excellence in the great national and scholarly libraries and the Codes based on their practice. And, as Hanson says, the primary requirement is for a system or scheme of knowledge, so that a subject inquiry can be fitted in and given a significance that turns it from a homeless bit of information into an item of real knowledge.

S. C. Bradford, whose pioneering book, *Documentation*, is the subject of Shera's second essay here, understood this well enough, and followed Paul Otlet and Henri La Fontaine in advocating the use of the Universal Decimal Classification for the arrangement of subject indexes and bibliographies. The UDC, based on Dewey's Classification, gives much greater opportunities for classifying in detail, not only through more division in the schedules but also through the devices supplied for linking together numbers from different parts of the schedules. The scheme grew out of bibliography, because Otlet and La Fontaine needed it for their enormous project of a universal card index of subjects; and it is significant that most of Bradford's own advocacy of UDC took place at meetings of the British Society for International Bibliography, which later merged with Aslib. A bibliography or subject index does not suffer from one major limitation of a library: it does not need to consider that the subject of a document must be given one place only in the arrangement, entries for the same work can be in several.

Thus the UDC, to a certain extent, if not completely, breaks away from its DC parent which *still* tries to list one place, and one only, for every subject that may be written about. It provides a flexible means of classifying, not only whole books and their broad subjects but bits of information, which may be contained in periodical articles, paragraphs, and even sentences. Though limited by the rigid structure of the DC basis, its auxiliary signs and schedules go far towards providing means for classifiers in individual libraries to compose class numbers that ensure an entry in the file for every aspect of a subject that concerns the library.

Characteristically, the UDC has had most success in special libraries, which serve groups of readers whose own interests cover all aspects of their subject field. This means that any one aspect may require to be searched for, to be used as the focal point towards which all other aspects are orientated. Special libraries thus require a form of index that can bring any aspect into the paramount position, showing other aspects as dependent, with the minimum of effort. This has two important consequences. First, it means a much higher proportion of indexing time to user time, and therefore more staff per reader; secondly, it means multiplying entries for any given document to the extent needed to cope with the multi-aspect approach.

In this age, such a proliferation of clerical work at once leads to the question: how far can these operations be mechanized? and perhaps it is here that Shera has shown his most acute perception. If in the United Kingdom we have been slow to appreciate what computer-type machines can offer, in the U.S.A. the pendulum has swung far in the other direction; the splendid performance of machines has dazzled many workers in this field, to such an extent, indeed, that the study of machine techniques has become an end in itself. Generous grants have been made available from various sources – not least the U.S. Government – for projects of undoubted interest, which generated further grant-attracting sub-projects, but which all too rarely ended in the practical operation of an information service. In circumstances so favourable to the proliferation of research, it has proved easy enough to lose sight of the important fact that, for us, the machine is a tool, and since we are not toolmakers, the design of machines does not concern us, except as users. It is up to the makers to produce machines to carry out the tasks we present; it is not up to us to distort our systems in order to provide work for machines designed to do something else.

From the very beginning of their work, Shera and his team at Western Reserve University have stressed this view. Following the example of Ralph Shaw and the Rapid Selector, they designed and built a machine for information retrieval, and at the same time set to work on the intellectual foundations of machine systems. The Semantic Code Index and the technique of semantic factoring offer a method for analysis in great depth of any text, ensuring consistency and catering for the multi-aspect approach of users. Their aim has been to show that the machines do not replace the intellectual skills of librarianship but enable them to be put to better use, because they can now grapple with the vastly increased quantities of information poured out by specialist research and publication. Classification, therefore, has a more vital rôle than ever, and those who, in the first flush of excitement over the potential of machine systems, discarded it altogether, have slowly and with great intellectual agony been finding their way back to it. The value of facet analysis, on the other hand, was early recognized in the development of the Semantic Code Index, and it has been used in several areas by members of the Center for Documentation and Communication Research.

The growth in popularity of the so-called 'thesaurus' approach illustrates both of these facts. The original *Thesaurus* of Roget was, in fact, an attempt to sort terms into categories, some of them very similar to the fundamental categories of Ranganathan: Relations, Space, Matter, Volition, for example. The alphabetical index brings together references to all the categories in which a single word may appear, in its various shades of meaning. It recognizes, in fact, that a term may have different connotations according to the context, in the same way as a term in the Colon Classification may appear in different facets according to the Main Class. In the United States, classification has for long been held in low repute, largely because of the rigid structure of the Decimal Classification, and still more of that of the Library of Congress. The alphabetical subject catalogue was held to overcome this rigidity simply because it allowed entries to appear under any term chosen by the indexer. It was inevitable, however, that some relationships would have to be built in, and a concealed classificatory base used. The 'thesaurus' represents a further step in this direction, by referring terms to categories based on a set of unifying ideas. Even so, some limit the term to the alphabetical index only, and do not provide the basic scheme, except by means of more or less systematic sets of cross-references.

The production of a 'thesaurus', however, does have a striking significance. The very fact that it is so called means that the compiler recognizes the need for controlling his indexing vocabulary by arranging it in *categories* of terms. Even if the categories are not shown, or if the terms in them are actually arranged alphabetically, the implication is still clear: a randomly chosen and uncontrolled set of terms in alphabetical order is inadequate as a retrieval system index. This inadequacy is well demonstrated by the Keyword-in-Context indexes which have been thunderously promoted as the answer to all retrieval problems. KWIC indexes use words in titles – an uncontrolled vocabulary; and one need only examine any KWIC index with modest care to see how far short of reasonable standards it falls – in random scattering of related terms, in ignoring synonyms, in wasteful use of unsought terms, and even in mystification due to the artificial limit imposed on the length of line. What is so dangerous about these indexes is that they are now estimated in terms of *production* and not of *use*; if a job represents an ingenious use of techniques of production, especially of computer techniques, it must be foisted upon us regardless of how inefficient and irritating it may be to use.

B

Shera's constant reiteration of the important point that computer techniques enable us to put more, and not less, intellectual effort into our indexes has had its effect. Although random or alphabetical sequences are still to be found, no one seriously maintains any longer that computers reduce input to retrieval systems to a mere clerical operation, and a new and interesting turn has been taken on the research level.

The same principles apply to the other aspect of documentation – the current awareness service. This requires two things: (1) knowledge of users' needs, and (2) the scanning of all new literature with these needs in mind. Once again, this has been difficult to achieve in the general library serving large numbers of readers, because of the quantity of transactions involved and the shortage of staff to carry them out. On the other hand, no change of principle enters, only an extension of existing methods. We already examine all new books and pamphlets in order to catalogue and classify them, that is, for their information content. Why should not the same examination suffice for information service? Why should not the examination be extended to issues of periodicals, indeed to documents of all kinds? It is this service that distinguishes the special library, and stems from its close association with its users. Such a close association can just as well exist in a general library; all that is required is staff of the right quality and quantity, and an efficient use of modern clerical equipment, or computers.

This will doubtless be expensive, but what of the alternative? Admitting that a proportion of what attains publication (in any field) may be rubbish, and not worth further attention from anybody, who can estimate the cost of repeating useful research that has already been done and published? Most of us, at some time, have heard a research worker lament his ignorance of a piece of published work that might have shortened or improved his own efforts. Access to information once published should no longer be so often a matter of chance. Research workers who publish, and research workers during their investigations, have the right to know that the middlemen of culture – the librarians – are actively engaged in the dissemination of information, and not merely looking after it in case someone, some day, may ask for it.

'Where is the information we have lost?' Shera's extension of

T. S. Eliot's questions underlines the importance of a current awareness service, for although information by itself is no more than tinkling cymbals, when presented to a prepared mind it becomes knowledge, and usable. And knowledge, refined by the experience of an individual in his life in society, becomes wisdom. The transformation depends on an active service to readers entering as an integral part of library operations. The WRU research teams recognize this, and have adopted the 'User Group' technique, by means of which all the results of research on retrieval methods are tested against real needs. This is more than an artificial arrangement in which search questions are 'concocted' on the basis of specific documents. The User Groups are sets of people who are actually engaged in advanced work in the field under investigation. The Group in the Education project includes teachers, administrators, psychologists, university and other research workers, and it is against the background of their actual needs that the Education documents at WRU are organized.

A similar method has been adopted by the National Electronics Research Council in London in its tests on the mechanization of a Selective Dissemination of Information service to industry. SDI based on such a national centre seems to offer a fruitful field of operations, and the director of the project, T. M. Aitchison, gave an interesting account of progress so far at the 1965 Conference of Aslib at the University of Keele. A successful introduction of automation at this stage in the flow of information might well effect a step forward comparable to the introduction of abstracts on a wide scale.

Documentation in the sense of current awareness and retrospective searching services has been the characteristic activity of special libraries in science and technology. The circumstances that brought it into existence are now coming about in other fields, notably in certain branches of the social sciences, but occasionally in the humanities as well. We already have *Modern Language Abstracts* and *English Teaching Abstracts*, and in his Chapter 7 Shera shows how automation offers new hope for the historian, who now, like the scientist before him, finds himself in danger of being overwhelmed by the mere mass of new information recorded and published. What is absolutely vital now is that these trends should be acknowledged, so that we can not only use the techniques forged in the documentation of science but also avoid the errors and duplications that have occurred there. When we have in our hands, for the first time, tools capable of handling even the present vast output right across the field of knowledge, it would be little short of infamous if we failed to take advantage of them, and allowed isolated efforts to spring up all unco-ordinated and wasteful as they are certain to be.

This work has been recognized by the Weinberg Committee on 'Science, government, and information' as being worthy of the attention of the best scientists, as important as laboratory work itself in the present state of science. This Committee laid particular stress on the value of what may be the highest form of information service – the narrative survey of the literature, covering a specific field and presented in such a way that it is acceptable to laymen as well as to specialists. With the increasing impact of science on our daily lives, the rôle of such presentation itself assumes a new validity, if we are to be informed, know-ledgeable and wise when taking decisions, at all levels. There is therefore a clear need for the recruitment of highly qualified people into the profession.

For we must never forget that this is a professional activity, the activity of professional librarians. Proper use of radically new techniques is impossible without a clear understanding of the rôle of the librarian and information officer in society. To pretend that mere equipment turns an activity into something else is to fall into the all-too-common heresy of thinking that men are made to serve machines, that production must be carried on at all costs, even if the rate quickens to the point when the product has to be discarded almost as soon as it is taken into service. The reverse is the case; but we must not fall either into the opposite error, of supposing that what was good enough in the nineteenth century will still serve today. A true understanding of our rôle in society will enable us to judge correctly the rôle of the machine, and to build on the centuries of service given by librarians to the cause of scholarship and progress; we shall not only cope, as we have done before, with mere increases in the output of documents, but also introduce new services appropriate to the needs of a new age.

Perhaps the most notable of Jesse Shera's many notable contributions to this profession has been his own personal demonstration of both the necessity and the possibility of achieving this ambition. The range of his scholarship and his keen sense of the practical prove that, as a profession, we need not rest content to follow in the footsteps of scholars; we can march at their side, and sometimes even lead them.

D. J. FOSKETT

1: *Documentation: Its Scope and Limitations*

THOUGH THE term 'documentation' is not of recent origin, attempts to define it precisely have been conspicuously unsuccessful. Usually, it has been described in such vague terms as 'a process by which are brought together, classified, and distributed, all the documents of all kinds of all the areas of human activity'. It was so understood by Paul Otlet, whose *Traité de documentation*[1] is now regarded as a classic discussion of the subject. The late S. C. Bradford closely followed Otlet by making of documentation 'the art of collecting, classifying and making readily accessible the records of all kinds of intellectual activity ... the process by which ... is ... put before the creative specialist the existing literature, bearing on the subject of his investigation, in order that he may be made fully aware of previous achievements in his subject, and thus be saved from the dissipation of his genius upon work already done'.[2] Kathrine Murra provisionally accepted the definition of the *Schweizer Lexikon*, which called it the 'handling and organization of scholarly materials'.[3] Egan and Shera avoided the issue by making documentation a part of what, on this side of the Atlantic, is usually understood as

---

[1] Paul Otlet, *Traité de documentation: Le Livre sur le livre, théorie et pratique* (Bruxelles: Editiones Mundaneum, 1934), pp. 6–8.

[2] S. C. Bradford, *Documentation* (London: Crosby Lockwood & Son, 1948), p. 11.

[3] Kathrine O. Murra, 'Second Interim Report of the UNESCO/Library of Congress Bibliographical Planning Group', 'Appendix, Library of Congress Information Bulletin' (September 13–19, 1949), p. 6. See also Leo M. Kern, *Grundfragen der Dokumentation* (Bern: Büchler & Co., 1948), pp. 3–5.

Paper presented at the U.S. Department of Agriculture, Washington, D.C., 1950. Originally published in *Library Quarterly*, Vol. 21 (January 1951), pp. 13–26.

'bibliographic control',[4] a term which, incidentally, they have rejected in favor of 'bibliographic organization'. Finally, one Yankee, hypersensitive to his professional status and with one eye on the roster of the Fédération Internationale de Documentation (hereafter referred to as 'FID' or 'International Federation for Documentation') and the other on the curriculum of the École des Chartes, has proclaimed documentation to be 'librarianship performed by amateurs'.

Yet from even these broad generalizations concerning the function of documentation, lacking in specificity though they be, it is possible to hypothesize about certain characteristics of documentation that will contribute to its definition. From the foregoing it seems clear that documentation is limited to that aspect of bibliographic organization which treats of the materials and needs of scholars and, hence, is concerned with the scholarly apparatus of bibliographies, indexes, and abstracting services. Therefore, documentation is to be regarded as an essential part of our modern system of graphic communication within the world of scholarship, an instrumental device to expedite the flow of recorded information *within* a group of specialists or *between* various groups of specialists. It is not concerned with the flow of communication at the popular, nonspecialist, or lay-public levels. Obviously, it is *not* concerned with the great bulk of the mass communication media, which are completely under the control of the transmitting agent, such as the radio, motion picture, or newspaper, *except* as such materials may have historical significance.

The essential task of documentation, then, may be described as the matching of two patterns: (*a*) the pattern of all scholarly activities in which the use of *primary* graphic records plays a part,' and (*b*) the pattern of intermediary services which transmit *primary* recorded materials from the scholar-as-producer to the scholar-as-user. By contrast, bibliographic organization is concerned with the channeling of graphic records to *all* users, for *all* purposes, and at *all* levels in such a way as to maximize the social utilization of recorded human experience.

Finally, documentation is *secondary* communication, in that it is not concerned with direct communication between specialist

[4] Margaret E. Egan and Jesse H. Shera, 'Prolegomena to Bibliographic Control', *Journal of Cataloging and Classification*, Vol. V (Winter, 1949), p. 17.

and specialist or, indeed, with communication within groups of specialists so small in number as to make any intermediary service unnecessary.[5] In summary, then, one may say that documentation is that portion of bibliographic organization that is involved with the *indirect* communication of *primary* materials within and among groups of specialists, to the end that they will receive, in a manner as efficient as possible, the data which they require for the effective execution of their work.

HISTORICAL SKETCH

To treat in any detail the complex history of documentation in Europe and America is obviously beyond the scope of the present paper;[6] nevertheless, there are certain 'landmark' agencies and services the importance of which cannot be ignored in even so brief a discussion as this. Such a survey should probably begin with the work of the Royal Society of London, which, during the years from 1851 to 1925, sought, through the publication of its *Catalogue of Scientific Papers*, to index the scientific periodicals of the nineteenth century. The result was an author list of scientific articles in the periodical literature of the past century, as well as subject indexes for pure mathematics, physics, and mechanics. The same society collaborated in the publication of *The International Catalogue of Scientific Literature*, the object of which was to prepare a subject index to the twentieth-century literature of seventeen branches of science but which was never carried beyond the year 1914. Both undertakings depended for their support upon subventions from the society and the British government, donations from individuals, and revenue from the sale of the materials themselves.

[5] For a fuller discussion of these definitions as applied to the processes of bibliographic organization see the Preface to 'Bibliographic Organization: Papers Presented before the Fifteenth Annual Conference of the Graduate Library School', published by the University of Chicago Press, 1951.

[6] For comprehensive treatments of the history of documentation see Kathrine O. Murra, 'Notes on the Development of the Concept of Current Complete National Bibliography', published as an appendix to the 'UNESCO/Library of Congress Bibliographical Survey' (Washington, 1950); also Kathrine O. Murra, 'History of Some Attempts To Organize Bibliography Internationally' in 'Bibliographic Organization: Papers Presented before the Fifteenth Annual Conference of the Graduate Library School'.

The *Concilium bibliographicum*, begun in 1895 and terminated in 1930, is of particular interest here as representing a bibliographic undertaking that was almost entirely the work of a single man, Dr Herbert Haviland Field, whose ambition was the international organization of the literature of zoology. The *Concilium* appeared as a bibliographic service in card form, classified according to its own elaborate expansion of the Dewey scheme. Later, a bibliographic index appeared in bulletin form. The project was supported by grants from the Swiss Confederation, the canton and city of Zürich, the Zoological Station at Naples, the American Association for the Advancement of Science, and numerous other sources, including the personal funds of Dr Field himself. The death of the founder in 1924 was a blow from which the venture never recovered – a dramatic example of how international bibliography should not be organized.

The best known of all the agencies for the encouragement of documentation is the organization founded in 1895 by Paul Otlet and Henri La Fontaine as the International Institute of Bibliography. Established under the auspices of, and with partial support from, the Belgian government, its original objective was fivefold: (1) to publish a journal that would serve as a medium for the exchange of information on bibliographic organization; (2) to serve as a clearing-house for bibliographic information; (3) to expand the Decimal Classification; (4) to establish a union catalog of world literature; and (5) to promote international meetings on bibliographic organization. In 1924 its character was changed from an international association of individual scholars to a federation of national groups, and in 1931 its official name became the International Institute for Documentation. Aided by gifts from the Royal Dutch Oil Company and the Rockefeller Foundation and by contributions from its affiliated organizations, it largely abandoned the original plan for a world documentation center and directed its attention toward the co-ordination of bibliographic services wherever they might be discovered. The publication of its official journal was continued, as was also its interest in expanding and encouraging the use of the Universal Decimal Classification. At frequent intervals, it sponsored international meetings on bibliographic organization. Six years later, in 1937, the name was again changed, this time to the International Federation for

Documentation, and its objective further restricted to the co-ordination of the activities of its member groups, though it did not abandon its paternal solicitude for the UDC. Its official publications are still an important source of information concerning the theory and practice of bibliographic organization, and it has maintained a continuing interest in the encouragement of international conferences; but it is perhaps best known (and most severely criticized in this country) for its vigorous promotion of the UDC. Today it is largely dependent for support upon the contributions of its affiliates, voluntary gifts from individual donors, and the sale of its publications. The American affiliate is, of course, the American Documentation Institute, which, only within recent months,* has begun the publication of its official organ, *American Documentation*, made possible by a grant from the Carnegie Corporation. Admittedly, the original dream of Otlet and La Fontaine for a world documentation center and bibliographic service has fallen far short of realization, but the FID is still an important force for the encouragement of organized bibliographic activity.

Other international organizations which sought to encourage bibliographic organization should be mentioned briefly. Between the years 1925 and 1946, the International Committee on Intellectual Co-operation, sponsored by the League of Nations, brought together subject specialists for the study of bibliographic problems in their respective fields, and in other ways studied and aided the better organization of literary, artistic, and scientific works. Perhaps its most tangible accomplishment was the publication, in 1925, of the *Index bibliographicus: An International Catalogue of Sources of Current Bibliographical Information* (*Periodicals and Institutions*), arranged and edited for the committee by Marcel Godet, director of the Swiss National Library, and revised in 1931. After a quarter of a century the work is still an important contribution to international bibliography. The committee also sponsored the International Institute of Intellectual Co-operation, which, with support from the French government, gave grants-in-aid for bibliographic work, including bibliographies, directories, journals, etc., and provided a forum for the discussion of bibliographic problems in subject fields.

* In 1950.

Beginning in 1927, the International Federation of Library Associations began a series of meetings at which information on library and bibliographic problems might be exchanged. It also sponsored the publication of the proceedings of these meetings as a permanent contribution to the literature of international bibliographic problems. Finally, at the present time, UNESCO is giving active support to the improvement of subject bibliography by giving grants-in-aid for bibliographic work in the area of international bibliography and is sponsoring international meetings to encourage the study of problems of international bibliographic organization and the search for solutions that would promote international co-operation in documentation.

One should not desert the international scene without mention of one organization, the Association of Special Libraries and Information Bureaux (Aslib), which, though not international in the sense characteristic of those previously mentioned, has, through its wholly admirable official organ, the *Journal of Documentation*, contributed greatly to the promotion of documentation far beyond its native England. Established in 1924 'to consider, promote and organize the systematic utilization of informational and library services', it was a British parallel to the American Special Libraries Association, though its membership included many directors of scientific and technical organizations as well as bibliographers and librarians of such agencies. Its financial support has come largely from the Carnegie United Kingdom Trust, with some assistance, since 1944, from the British government. Its major contribution to international bibliography may probably be dated from 1945, when it began the sponsorship of the previously mentioned *Journal of Documentation* under the editorship of Theodore Besterman. Its international ties were further strengthened in 1948, when it absorbed the British Society for International Bibliography, the English affiliate of FID.

At the national level, documentation in America may be conveniently classified into four major categories, according to the source from which it derives the bulk of its support.

1. *The federal government.* Ever since the days of Charles C. Jewett and the early years of the Smithsonian Institution, the federal government has recognized the importance of documentation and has taken some steps toward its encouragement. Conspicuous examples are the Union Catalog of the Library of

Congress, which was initiated by a foundation grant; the *Bibliography of Agriculture*, issued by the library of the Department of Agriculture and an outstanding example of bibliographic achievement; the several special bibliographies issued by the Census Library Project, a joint undertaking of the Library of Congress and the Bureau of the Census; the Index-Catalogue of the Army Medical Library; the numerous regional union catalogs developed largely by assistance from the Works Progress Administration; *Writings on American History*, an annual publication sponsored by the American Historical Association but receiving financial aid from government funds; and the bibliographic publications of the Library of Congress.

2. *Learned societies, professional associations, and academic institutions.* One would do well to consider the three types of agencies as a single unit, inasmuch as more than one are frequently involved in a single undertaking. Here might be cited *Chemical Abstracts*, sponsored by the American Chemical Society; *Engineering Index*, sponsored by the American Society of Mechanical Engineers co-operating closely with the Engineering Societies Library of New York; other abstracting services which tended to follow the pattern set by *Chemical Abstracts* (e.g., *Biological Abstracts* and *Psychological Abstracts*); *Population Index*; and the late lamented *Social Science Abstracts*.

3. *Commercial enterprises.* In general, bibliography has not proved to be a commercially profitable undertaking, and libraries will, of course, think of the work of the H. W. Wilson Company as being the prime example of the successful commercialization of bibliography. However, the broader concept of documentation would include such commercial services as those issued by the Commerce Clearing House, the McGraw-Hill Publishing Company, and the legal services designed to facilitate the use of the rapidly expanding and increasingly intricate body of law.

4. *Special libraries.* The entire special library movement is, of course, an implicit acknowledgement on the part of industry and business of the fact that the organization of documentation for the use of its research and administrative personnel is economically profitable to private enterprise. This is especially true for industrial research, where the organization of private research reports is a vital problem in documentation.

Even this cursory history of documentation is sufficient to

make certain conclusions abundantly clear: (1) A real social need for documentation has been recognized by widely divergent groups, representing disparate subject interests and bibliographic requirements; (2) attempts at the solution of problems of documentation have largely languished in 'intellectual isolation', ignorance of contemporaneous developments in other areas, and disregard of previous errors that a better knowledge of history might have prevented; (3) documentation can be successful – and conspicuously so – when its organization and management are based on thorough understanding of the needs to be met and the resources available; (4) successful documentation demands the co-ordination of all resources – intellectual, organizational, and economic; (5) leadership in the promotion of documentation is already widely recognized as a proper responsibility of the federal government; and (6) far too much time and money have been wasted in unprofitable discussion which has failed to result either in searching investigation of the problems to be solved or in constructive action within even the limited range of our present knowledge. With these lessons of history clearly before us, let us examine more closely the character of documentation itself.

APPROACHES TO DOCUMENTATION

Types of Users

There are two possible major approaches to the problems of documentation: (1) by type of user, and (2) by agency or organizational unit. In large measure the two are closely interrelated and even interdependent, though, for the sake of clarity, they will here be dealt with separately. One should also add that it is desirable to consider the types of users in terms of the properties and *forms* of the literature that they need and now have available to them, as well as by the *type* of information with which they are concerned.

Pure scientists. The characteristic of the literature which is of primary interest to the pure scientists (e.g., physicists, chemists, and astronomers) is that it records the establishment of a new fact or cluster of facts, a new relationship among facts previously known, or a new method for the manipulation of techniques or data already known. Hence, the scientist needs *comprehensive* and *primary* materials for the results (factual findings) that they set forth, for verification of those findings, or for the presentation of the method which he may possibly apply, with or without modifications, to the problems in which he himself is immediately concerned. He needs not only single, isolated facts (the atomic weight of a newly discovered element, for example) but *all* facts of a given class (i.e., the atomic weights of all the elements) for bases of comparison and relationship. In addition, he requires easy access to all established *descriptive* facts about one particular element, compound, or substance, such as the physical and chemical properties of aluminium, of the halides of silver, or of a newly developed alcohol. Finally, he needs access to the literature of all *problems* that have been approached through the application of a particular *method* or through a particular *principle*, *hypothesis*, or *law*. He may be as much interested in the reporting of failures or partial successes as in verified results. Because the research materials that the pure scientist needs are primary and unique and do not permit of substitution, his bibliographic requirements call for a *comprehensive* index of the *entirety* of the primary literature of research that falls within the limits of his subject field. The internal arrangement of that literature, its classification, indexing, subject grouping, etc., must permit approaches to it by type of material dealt with, by the physical and chemical 'environment' of the reaction, by results of investigation, by method employed, and by any other possible groupings that may be meaningful to him.

In addition to the specific bibliographic needs of his immediate purposes, the pure scientist must be kept informed of activities in related areas of research. Here his requirements are much less exhaustive and precise, in that he does not need to be conversant with every experiment or with every detail of every account in which he may have a general interest. In such areas the best service for him may be the bibliographic essay. Such essays are surveys or summaries of the more important bibliographic contributions in specified problem areas and tend to emphasize the interrelationships of the several parts with the whole and to delineate the importance of such contributions in and to peripheral subject areas.

The interests in the separate subject fields of the pure sciences are so divergent and the bibliographic requirements of the specialists working in these disciplines so varied that no single bibliographic service can be made to serve all of them. Hence arises the demand for separate services in such fields as chemistry, physics, mathematics, etc. Furthermore, these indexes should be retrospective and should be cumulated at frequent intervals. They are *collective*, or library, tools designed to meet the bibliographic problems of groups of scientists using the literature largely in library situations, whether these libraries be subject departments in large public, academic (i.e., college and university), or special libraries created specifically for the use of the research staff of an industrial organization. By contrast, the bibliographic essay needs revision rather than cumulation and is designed primarily for individual, rather than for collective, use.

Technicians. The second major group of users of documentation are the technicians, a class composed of engineers, mechanics, inventors, and manufacturers. Their needs are sharply contrasted with those of the pure scientists, in that they are primarily concerned with the *results* of research rather than the materials, methods, or verifications of the experimental process. The established facts with which the technicians deal, though they may emanate from the work of the pure scientists, can be in large part derived from *secondary* sources, such as manuals, handbooks, guides, trade catalogs, and similar compilations of data. But there are times, particularly when work is being done in fields characterized by the rapid discovery of new data, when the technicians, too, must have access to the *primary* literature of pure science. In such cases they would, of course, make use of the documentation services employed by the pure scientists.

The technician must also have readily available the large body of literature that reports the activities of his colleagues in identical or related technologies. Such literature is characteristically experiential and descriptive; it reports to the reader the development of a new process, the solution to problems encountered in a new installation, or the characteristics of a new mechanism. In the purest sense it is *instrumental*, in that it gives to the engineer, for example, a case history of the construction of a new type of dam, the technical data on a new steam turbine, the operating characteristics of a new vacuum tube or electronic relay. Such materials present a factor of *exchangeability* which is not to be found in the research literature of pure science, and access need not be exhaustive. The hydraulic engineer may wish to study the case histories of the construction of a number of dams that seem to present problems similar to those by which he is confronted, but he certainly feels no compulsion to pore over the history of the building of every dam that was ever constructed. Likewise, he may find that the reporting of experiences in certain kinds of non-dam construction will be very pertinent to his own work. Thus bibliographic guides to this experiential literature should be highly selective, but its internal arrangement and organization should admit of a variety of approaches: by materials employed, by methods used, by place where construction has been effected, and by climate, temperature, or other physical factors which might conceivably have a bearing on the results. The classification of patent literature is an excellent case in point, in which it is necessary to organize a vast and complex literature according to structure, function or effect, and the 'art' involved.

The technician, like the pure scientist, finds it necessary to keep abreast of new developments in his own and related fields, but for this purpose the substantive journal of a profession or trade is probably a more effective medium than a bibliographic service. Though this is largely a personal rather than a bibliographic or documentation problem, it should be pointed out that the ways in which technicians make use of this substantive literature are important to the organizational problems of documentation and need much more investigation and study than they have received in the past. Certain journals, such as *Nature* or *Science*, admit of, and are typographically so arranged as to encourage, reasonably thorough and careful study. Other publications, like the *Journal of the American Chemical Society*, each issue of which is bulky, relatively cumbersome, and closely printed, are seldom, if ever, read 'from cover to cover' but are consulted only when relevant materials are cited elsewhere. Technical and trade publications, by contrast, are often characterized by comparatively slight and unimportant substantive or editorial matter but contain a very substantial bulk of advertising, which is heavily used by technicians as a quick and easy source of information concerning new technical developments. From a careful analysis of the professional reading habits of both pure scientists and technicians, important data may be obtained that would contribute to the solution of problems in documentation.

In existing situations the line of demarcation between pure

c

scientists and technicians is often not easily distinguishable; at times each group may operate in the manner of the other, and the functions of both are not infrequently combined in the work of a single individual. For our immediate purposes, the need for clarity and simplification has dictated a sharpening of boundaries that may well be regarded as somewhat over-emphatic. Also, what has been said here about the requirements of scholars and technicians in the physical sciences applies equally to social scientists and even, to some extent, to the humanists. In the social sciences the distinction between pure scientist and technician is frequently very ill-defined indeed. The physical scientists, therefore, have been chosen as an example, partly because their methods of operation may be described with greater precision, and partly for the reason that they, more than the other groups, have effectively developed the bibliographic services of their discipline.

Educators and students. The bibliographic needs of the educator and the student at the level of professional preparation are not unlike those of both the preceding groups, depending, of course, upon the character of the research pursued or the course of study involved. Suffice it here to point out that every graduate student should be made fully conscious of the purposes and limitations of the documentary services and bibliographic tools in his area of specialization, and that all professional preparation for advanced degrees should include adequate instruction in the relevant sources of bibliographic information. Only through such pedagogic methods can personnel be trained who will at once be skilled in the requisite bibliographic resources and fully conscious of the importance of documentation to the effective prosecution of their work. Failure to meet this important need in the past has been due partly to a general neglect or disregard of its values and partly to a shortage of instructional staff adequately prepared in documentation. Future provision of such bibliographic specialists trained to give instruction in subject bibliography might well become a responsibility of the library schools, working in close co-operation with the subject departments of the universities of which they are a part.

The layman. By definition, the bibliographic needs of the lay public have been excluded from the area of service of documentation and reserved for that larger sphere of activity here denominated 'bibliographic organization'. Nevertheless, it is relevant to emphasize that, if a popular climate of opinion favorable to the acceptance of new developments in science and technology and affirmatively disposed toward the use of public funds for the support of scientific inquiry and research is to be encouraged, the public must be kept informed of the importance of such scientific developments through popularizations that will interpret the social utility of science in lay terms. This is particularly important if government agencies continue to engage more and more in research and technologic experimentation and if government resources are to be increasingly used to finance private investigation. Popularization of the findings of research, in both the physical and the social sciences, thus takes its proper place as an important contribution to the entire democratic process.

For the writer of 'popularizations' the bibliographic essay is the most useful bibliographic service, yet it is also frequently the most inaccessible. Because it is a synthesis designed primarily to give the individual a survey of significant developments in a particular field rather than a guide to specific citations, librarians do not recognize the bibliographic essay as a special form and do not usually indicate it as such; hence it is in constant danger of being lost in the mass of journal articles which are customarily indexed by subject according to the principle of specific entry. This bibliographic problem for the popularizer is further complicated by the fact that the bibliographic essay is not a primary, but a secondary, form of bibliographic organization. It is the capstone of the pyramid of bibliographic organization, which cannot be set in place until an adequate supporting structure of prerequisite bibliographic services has been firmly erected.

Types of Agencies

Historically, libraries antedated the development of documentation services or even the publication of bibliographic tools. Ancient, medieval, and even relatively modern libraries were vast storehouses of accumulated records with the most crude and meager of bibliographic devices to reveal the wealth of their resources. However, differentiation among libraries according to the groups they served developed early and in the nineteenth century had attained a relatively advanced stage. This very differentiation of function was in itself a form of bibliographic service, a kind of bibliographic specialization that was a crude response to the bibliographic requirements of diversified groups of interests. But it had the unfortunate effect of scattering library resources among a wide variety of library types. Hence arose our contemporary motley pattern of documentation, grown to elephantine bulk, without plan, organization, or integration – a chaos in which vast and important areas of bibliographic activity are neglected, institutional competition abounds, the cross-fertilization of subject disciplines is ignored, and economic and social waste is rampant.

The second major approach to the problem of documentation, then, may well be made through a consideration of certain of these types of library agencies which service our present system of documentation.

Large research libraries. Research libraries naturally emerged from the book collections which were assembled to support the work of the universities. This was a logical and spontaneous development because, for centuries, the universities themselves were the most important agency for the promotion of research and inquiry. But in part it was also a consequence of the growth of the book collection. Relatively small libraries are adequate to most non-research needs, but, as libraries grew in size and the extent of their book resources tended to exceed the needs of more 'popular' book use, certain public libraries began to attract the patronage of those making special investigations and hence, almost without conscious choice, began to take on the characteristics and responsibilities of documentation agencies supporting the non-academic, as well as the academic, research program. Thus did such public libraries as those of New York, Boston, and Cleveland grow to the stature of research libraries. So also did the Library of Congress, shortly after the turn of the century, come to be regarded not only as a great national bibliographic center for the benefit of the government but as an engine of scholarship in a wide variety of fields. Even in this broad and often undefined area, specialization began to appear, for the academic libraries, which attracted their clientele largely from their own academic communities, soon began to adjust their acquisition policies to the specific pattern of the parent-institution. Thus, though the library of the University of Chicago and that of the Massachusetts Institute of Technology are both important research collections, the character of their respective holdings is remarkably dissimilar. This trend toward specialization was further intensified by the establishment of independent research libraries, such as the Huntington, Folger, John Crerar, and Newberry, which often began from private, personal collections of a single individual, in which bibliographic function was sharply and very specifically defined. Such definition is not contingent upon the needs of a parent-institution, since none exists, but is largely fortuitous, resulting from the nature of the initial collection, the terms of a bequest, and the needs of its clientele as envisaged by the administrative staff.

Storage libraries. The rapid growth of the collections of research libraries has begun to necessitate a second important step in the documentation of research, the establishment of the centralized co-operative storage library. The first such agency was established in 1941, in the environs of Cambridge, Massachusetts, as the New England Deposit Library, though a proposal for such an undertaking had been made many years before by President Charles W. Eliot of Harvard, following an earlier suggestion for storage facilities made by the Harvard librarian, William Coolidge Lane.[7] Today the most conspicuous example is the founding of the Midwest Inter-Library Center in Chicago (MILC), which will draw its materials from more than a dozen co-operating institutions. Originally, these deposit libraries were little more than warehouses for the storage of infrequently consulted materials for research, but special bibliographic techniques for their particular servicing problems are being considered, as well as plans for the development of their own acquisition policies and program. It is not inconceivable that, in time, they may become true documentation centers, equipped with many kinds of special bibliographic apparatus designed to meet their specialized requirements, i.e., co-ordinating agencies that will do much to eliminate duplication and waste, direct attention to neglected areas, and discourage institutional rivalry.[8]

Special libraries. Special libraries have often been regarded as an American invention, if not specifically the brain child of John

[7] Francis X. Doherty, 'The New England Deposit Library', *Library Quarterly*, Vol. 18, pp. 245–254.
[8] See Ernest Cadman Colwell, 'Co-operation or Suffocation', *College and Research Libraries*, Vol. X (July 1949), pp. 195–198, 207.

Cotton Dana. Actually, however, comparable agencies of documentation have flourished in England and on the Continent as information bureaus, documentation centers, and the like. Characteristically, they are working collections, supported by the purest type of documentation service, for a numerically small group of specialists who frequently have potentially very wide interests. The special library can operate most efficiently if its collection of primary materials is kept to a minimum, while it is free to draw upon the resources of larger collections for additional needs. Basic to its working collection are the bibliographic services of those fields potentially relevant to its own clientele. Obviously, it must be staffed by personnel trained in the use of these tools and capable of manipulating them intelligently for the procuring of additional sources of information through inter-library loan, reprint, photostat, or microfilm, as dictated by need. One scarcely need labor the point that substantive training in the fields of specialization is as essential to adequate staff performance as competence in the skills of documentation.

Such libraries, particularly those affiliated with the major industries, are increasingly being called upon to maintain and service, as part of their collections, the confidential research reports produced by the parent-organization. Such reports, because they customarily record patentable information or data which, for other reasons, must be kept securely within the official family of the organization, constitute a real barrier in the flow of communication within the system of documentation. Under our present economy of private enterprise, one can scarcely criticize an industrial corporation for wishing to keep to itself the results of its own research which give it an advantage over its competitors; at the same time, such restrictions on freedom of communication should be recognized as being potentially a grave social problem and one of the social costs that must be paid if we are to maintain our adherence to 'free competition'.

The more ambitious special libraries, such as the Army Medical Library and the library of the United States Department of Agriculture, not only attempt to assemble definitive collections in their respective fields, the collection to be serviced by a highly qualified staff, but they frequently assume responsibility for the publication of bibliographic guides to the literature of their particular subject areas. Such a combination of an extensive collection, trained personnel, and an integrated bibliographic service represents the best possible allocation of responsibility in subject bibliography – our nearest approach to the documentation ideal. Such agencies, however, should always be publicly owned, responsive to social needs, and accessible to all potential users on a free or 'at-cost' basis. Adequate bibliographic planning should look forward to the expansion of such meritorious undertakings into many more subject fields and at state and regional as well as national levels. The regional agencies, perhaps, might well be organized as branches of the national service.

Bibliographic centers. The bibliographic center emerged as an adjunct of the municipal, state, or regional union catalog, which had their period of greatest expansion during the years when the Works Progress Administration was seeking outlets for public expenditure in which labor costs were relatively high in relation to total overhead. As mere union catalog, arranged alphabetically by author as finding tools only, without regard to subject analysis, they were aids to physical rather than to content accessibility. But in certain instances, notably Philadelphia, Denver, and Seattle, a wide variety of special services in documentation were added to the simple one of locating materials. Though there may be real danger in the unco-ordinated multiplication of union lists and comparable attenuated bibliographic services, especially at the local level, one can scarcely deny that a limited number of well-planned and judiciously distributed bibliographic centers could greatly improve existing resources in documentation. Furthermore, the fact that the withdrawal of government subsidy has brought financial crises to many of these centers again substantiates the contention that documentation is basically a social responsibility, the costs of which should be met from public funds, the planning for which should be on a national scale, and the services of which should be available to all.

Other (non-institutional) instruments of documentation. The non-institutional instruments of documentation include a wide and completely disorganized array of published bibliographic materials. Their excellence varies greatly from field to field and from sponsoring agency to sponsoring agency. They may evince the high standard of scholarship of *Chemical Abstracts*, *Psychological Abstracts*, or *Population Index*. They may be the result of the initiative of a professional association, a learned society, an educational institution, or an overtly commercial enterprise. They may exist as comprehensive independent services, bibliographic addenda to professional journals issued at stipulated or more or less regular intervals, bibliographic essays and reviews of work in progress published at completely irregular and often idiosyncratic time periods. Of all the forms of documentation, these are the most chaotic and least integrated and stand in greatest need of study and research before co-ordination and planning are possible. Finally, even the best and most scholarly of these instruments of documentation largely ignore the problem of the location of the materials of which they treat, a limitation which in itself results in a truncated bibliographic service. This assertion is not intended to imply that such services should combine both subject and physical accessibility, for it may well be that the two should be kept largely separate; but, at least, the problem should be recognized and the limitations which existing policies dictate fully understood.

Internal Arrangement

Though the internal arrangements (organization) of documentation services are the very key to their success, the fragmentary and chaotic growth of the existing system of documentation, if it has not actually discouraged a solution to this problem, has at least not contributed to its solution. To be sure, there have been repeated attempts to standardize the form of bibliographical entry, and there are many who would gladly promote a general acceptance of the UDC; nevertheless, anyone who has ever tried to cumulate the citations of a single service or interfile the entries of even a limited number of different services must realize how far we are from standardization even in those limited areas where general agreement may be relatively easy to achieve. There is no virtue in uniformity for the sake of uniformity, and, admittedly, varying types of materials and varying subject approaches necessitate corresponding variations in organization and treatment. Yet the possibility of multiple bibliographic services designed to meet differing needs of various groups, but emanating from a single centralized source, is certainly the most economical and effective way of achieving adequate bibliographic coverage.

At the present time the profession lacks an appropriate tool or technique for the effective internal arrangement of existing or future documentation services. There is no method for bringing under control the growing mass of documentation which must be properly channeled if waste and inefficiency in scholarship are to be avoided. But it is at least a hopeful sign that interest in classification and other problems relevant to internal arrangement is on the increase and that new mechanical and electronic devices, which depend for their success upon the effectiveness of the classification systems they employ, are near at hand. The problems, then, of internal arrangement, or classification, are the ones to which we must address ourselves – by the thorough investigation of the approaches to documentation, the manner in which scholars arrive at the documentary sources they need, the uses they make of the materials they find, and the sources of failure in the existing system of scholarly communication. Specifically, this means a better understanding of the thought unit and its use in scholarly activity, of the extent to which organized bibliography brings the arrangement of its materials into juxtaposition with the thought unit, and of the relation between the thought unit and the graphic unit with the goal of making the two essentially one. By the 'thought unit' is meant a concept or constellation of concepts meaningful to the scholar-as-user; the 'graphic unit' is its counterpart in graphic form. The concept 'tree' may be resolved, for example, into either its properties as lumber for the forester or its horticultural characteristics for the landscape architect. Each such resolution of the essence 'tree' is a thought unit, and the task of documentation is the effective matching of such concepts to their appropriate expressions in literature (whether such an expression be the current market price per board-foot of white pine, f.o.b. Duluth, or the acid-soil requirements of mountain laurel). It is the degree to which this matching process approaches coincidence of thought unit with graphic unit that determines the effectiveness of the organization of the documentation service, whether that organization be applied to a shelf of books, a card catalog, a printed bibliography, a sequence of photographic facsimiles on microfilm, or an electronic sorter with the data itself.

In conclusion, documentation lies at the very heart of librarianship, and the primary responsibility of the librarian is to make of himself an expert in bibliographic organization. He is not a 'keeper' of the records of the human adventure against the ravages of time; nor is he the presiding officer of a 'people's university'. Certainly, he is not an executive who orders the professional lives of subordinates for the pure joy of practicing administrative theory. Rather, he is a bibliographer in the widest and wisest possible sense, a practitioner of bibliographic organization. Let librarians, then, apply themselves to the problems of bibliographic organization, become once more the acknowledged leaders in the largely uncharted world of subject bibliography, and, in the stern discipline of documentation, not only achieve a new professional self-respect but rediscover their true purpose in society.

2: *A Review of the Present* State of *Librarianship and Documentation*

WHEN, IN the summer of 1947, S. C. Bradford brought together in book form under the title *Documentation* a collection of essays treating of the problems of making available to scholarship the sum total of the results of human work and thought, the book became not only the definitive but the only substantial treatment of the subject in the English language. Reviewers were unanimous, and properly so, in comparing it to Paul Otlet's monumental *Traité de documentation* (published in 1934) and the first part of Frank's *Die Decimal Klassifikation*, which was published in Berlin just one year prior to Bradford's synthesis. Although for over half a century the fundamental principles of documentation had slowly been evolving from the practices of workers in the field, no precise and comprehensive textbook on the subject had been written, and it was in response to this general need that Bradford was encouraged by his colleagues to set about this task.

In the six years that have elapsed since Bradford began the assembly and organization of his materials his work has remained unchallenged by any other English treatment of similar magnitude, and on the Continent only the recently published *Qu'est-ce que la Documentation?* by Madame Suzanne Briet can be regarded as a possible competitor.

But Bradford's *Documentation* has a subtle importance that far transcends its primacy. Bradford was not only a 'documentalist' in the restricted and technical sense but in addition he was a scientist and a librarian, and thus he is himself a symbol of the real unity that brings together under the comprehensive

---

With Margaret E. Egan. Originally published in S. C. Bradford, *Documentation*, 2nd edition (London: Crosby Lockwood, 1953), pp. 11–45.
* Although this was written twelve years ago, the use of this adjective is still justified!

term 'bibliographic organization' the professional interests and activities of both documentalists and librarians – a unity that is given substance and precision by being founded upon scientific training. The book, then, can be properly regarded as a milestone in the development of both documentation and librarianship, all the more important because it demonstrates the community of interests and problems through which the two can develop a conscious unity of purpose.

That librarianship and documentation are a unity is the major thesis of this introductory statement. Admittedly, in recent decades, documentation and librarianship have tended to separate. This has resulted from a variety of causes. The librarians, on their part, have not remained true to their professional objectives but have inclined to wander away in a wide variety of peripheral activities which were alluring but inappropriate to the inherent nature of their responsibilities. The documentalists have not seen that their operations were founded in the practice of librarianship, and have been unwilling to profit from the errors and achievements of their colleagues in the library field. Superficially, the historical development of the two disciplines has tended to obscure the bonds through which the two are united, though a more careful examination of their respective histories supplies the most powerful of arguments for their essential oneness. To make this clear it is necessary to examine in some detail the historical evolution of both disciplines, emphasizing as the treatment progresses the vast areas in which there has been true community of effort and identity of purpose.

HISTORICAL DEVELOPMENT

The origins of the term 'documentation' as used in the technical sense by Bradford are obscure. The *Oxford English Dictionary* does not include it as one of the definitions listed therein, though it does quote the complaint of a writer in the *Westminster Gazette* of July 4, 1895, to the effect that 'there is so much to read up, so much documentation to be exercised'. Doubtless, as a technical term it was first introduced, at the end of the last century, by those who, like Paul Otlet and Henri La Fontaine, were concerned with the promotion of universal bibliography at the international level.

But there is no novelty about documentation as a discipline for the organizing of graphic records. Bibliographies of a restricted scope appeared long before the age of the manuscript came to an end. As far back as the second century Galen found it necessary to compile a classified bibliography of his writings. In A.D. 731 the Venerable Bede appended to his *Ecclesiastical History of Britain* a list of some forty works arranged in a roughly classified order. In the main, however, the bibliographic compilations of the era before the invention of printing were bio-bibliographies of Christian churchmen like the *Catalogus scriptorum ecclesiæ* of John Boston of Bury (fl. 1400) in which the compiler recorded the titles of the books he found in the libraries of the monasteries and other ecclesiastical houses of England. This union list included materials drawn from no less than 195 such repositories and was arranged alphabetically by author, followed by a partial classification of the writers under the several books of the Bible about which they had written.[1] Thus subject bibliography, the early manifestation of documentation, is almost as old as the practice of librarianship itself, and in the beginning the one was quite indistinguishable from the other. Libraries began as simple storehouses of books and manuscripts, but with the introduction of printing and the resultant tremendous increase in the accumulation of graphic materials, it soon became apparent that mere acquisition was insufficient and that organization of this accumulated record was essential, even mandatory, if the stores of books were to fulfil any social purpose. Thus crude classification, or, more precisely, rough subject arrangements of the books themselves were devised, and this was followed, not long thereafter, by the compilation of subject bibliography. Documentation, then, has its roots deep in librarianship, and may be said to have begun when, at the end of the fifteenth century, Johann Tritheim compiled his *Liber de Scriptoribus Ecclesiasticis* and his *Catalogus Illustrium Virorum Germani*, and, half a century later, Konrad Gesner prepared his *Bibliotheca Universalis*, the first attempt at a universal bibliography. In this last work, a folio of thirteen hundred pages, were listed, with annotations, approximately twelve thousand titles, all the Latin, Greek, and Hebrew books known to the compiler. The

---

[1] Theodore Besterman, *The Beginnings of Systematic Bibliography* (Oxford: Oxford University Press, 1935), pp. 2–6.

arrangement of this work was alphabetical by the Christian names of the authors, but it was followed three years later by the *Pandectarum sive Partitionum Universalium*, in which the titles were rearranged according to some twenty major classes, though medicine and theology were never published.

The works of Tritheim and Gesner were followed by a great proliferation of subject bibliographies and catalogues of particular library collections, but the significant fact is that by the end of the sixteenth century the bulk of recorded literature was already so great that scholars felt the need for some systematization of it. Trade bibliographies, the precursors of national bibliography, particularly the lists of books on sale at the trade fairs, should also be mentioned, but they were inappropriate for scholarly use because of the almost accidental nature of the titles included and the lack of subject arrangement. Modern problems of bibliographic organization, then, are at least as old as the printed book itself, and they became increasingly intense with each change in the volume and nature of publication.

Thus for more than four centuries librarianship was almost synonymous with bibliography and the progenitors of the modern public library movement saw the problems of improving the techniques of bibliographic organization as central to the practice of librarianship itself. Indeed, libraries themselves came to depend more and more upon bibliography as an essential aid to their book acquisition programme. The growth in the literature of human experience and the multiplication of libraries brought with it an increasing refinement of the techniques of library and bibliographic organization. In Britain the formulation, in 1841, of the famous 'ninety-one rules' laid the foundation for library cataloguing practice for generations to come. A decade later, across the Atlantic, Charles C. Jewett and his contemporaries urged the creation at the Smithsonian Institution of a great national bibliographic and documentation centre, proposed, at the first American library conference, in 1853, a union catalogue of the holdings of all the major American libraries, and in a variety of ways demonstrated their conviction that the improvement of existing techniques for the bibliographic organization of library materials was fundamental to improved library practice. These same techniques were further substantially advanced when, in 1876, Melvil Dewey published the first edition of his

Decimal Classification, the first major library and documentation classification system to be widely adopted, and at the same time Charles Ammi Cutter compiled his *Rules for a Dictionary Catalogue*, which still remains one of the best treatments of subject cataloguing that the profession has produced. Shortly thereafter the Library of Congress began to assume leadership in bibliographic organization through the development of its classification scheme and its extensive system for the distribution of uniform printed catalogue cards.

Also significant in the history of documentation is the growing importance of the periodical as a medium of publication. By the middle of the nineteenth century the journal had a history of almost two centuries, but by 1850 its importance to scholarship had grown so great that librarians were convinced that some technique must be devised for the subject organization of its contents. In 1848 *An Alphabetical Index to Subjects Treated in the Reviews and other Periodicals* was issued under the auspices of the Brothers in Unity Library of Yale University. As its compiler, William Frederick Poole, explained in the introduction:

> Although we have every General Index that has been issued by the publishers of the several Reviews and Magazines, yet several hundred volumes of Standard Periodicals in our Library are comparatively useless as works of reference, from the want of proper Indexes. Nearly all these have been issued within the last twenty years, and contain the most elaborate discussions of those questions that have interested the literary and political world.[2]

By the time of the first conference of the American Library Association, in 1876, the subject control of periodical literature had become an even more serious problem. At the fourth session of these meetings Poole reported that a new edition of his index would be much too burdensome for the efforts of a single man, and there was general enthusiasm for inter-library co-operation to revive the project.[3] The Smithsonian had just published a

[2] P. iii. William F. Poole, comp., *An Alphabetical Index to Subjects Treated in the Reviews and Other Periodicals to which no Indexes have been Published*. Prepared for the Library of the Brothers in Unity, Yale College. New York: George P. Putnam, 1848.

[3] Proceedings of the Conference, *Library Journal*, Vol. 1, no. 2 (November 30, 1876), pp. 112–115.

revision of its *Catalogue of Publications of Societies . . . Belonging to the Smithsonian Institution*, and was shortly to issue as a supplement its *Catalogue of Scientific Periodicals, not Issued by Societies, from 1665 to 1874*. Finally, a number of librarians reported that they were being compelled to prepare their own periodical indexes, a service which they could not long maintain. Thus was begun a general movement for the subject analysis of periodical literature, and it must be noted that in its initial stages this analysis was recognized to be a legitimate library function.

The reasons for the later failure to continue this service are not far to seek. Perhaps the fundamental reason lies in the organizational structure of libraries themselves. Libraries had developed as local, autonomous agencies, built upon the premise that each community could own all the books that its citizens needed and that the organizational machinery within each such library would be sufficient to ensure access to the contents of the local library. In other words, *physical* access and *content* access were to be provided upon a purely local basis.

The second major reason for the breakdown of the library's machinery for providing content access lies in the rapid development of the journal as an important form of publication. Both the library catalogue and the library classification scheme had been based upon the book, or monograph, as the accepted, almost universal, bibliographic unit. By contrast, the journal is a composite of many bibliographic units, each article constituting a separate entity, yet all physically united as a volume or series of volumes regardless of the intellectual diversity of the content. Library classification systems, intended to bring together in physical contiguity materials of similar content, broke down completely when confronted by the problems arising from the proliferation of journals. In theory, the library catalogue might have continued to provide subject access by making catalogue entries for each separate article, but in practice libraries lacked both the personnel and the financial resources to maintain such a burdensome process. At the same time, the very fact that the contents of journals were the same for all libraries which subscribed to them made them amenable to centralized analysis in a way that books had never been. Co-operative indexing was possible, and was indeed attempted, but the machinery for co-ordinating such a project among many independent and widely separated libraries was too cumbersome to be practicable. The professional immaturity of library organization at that time prevented the establishment of a centralized indexing service supported by contributions from the institutional members.

Thus, an important part of the bibliographic mechanism for providing content access to a large body of contemporary literature passed out of the hands of the library profession and, in so far as this material was concerned, the library was reduced to its older function of physical custodianship. This abandonment of an important and previously well-recognized part of professional responsibility not only weakened the prestige of the library profession in relation to other professional groups but, more important, immeasurably weakened and stultified the growth of the intellectual discipline of librarianship. That segment of librarianship which had thus been sloughed off was picked up and developed by the growing group of documentalists.

Such library pioneers as Edwards and Panizzi in Britain and Jewett, Winsor, Cutter, and Poole in the United States had seen, in the provision of the bibliographic machinery necessary to provide both physical and subject access to printed records, the real social purpose of the library. It remained for their successors to reject a considerable part of this primary responsibility and to take up, in a futile attempt to rehabilitate their professional prestige, aims and objectives which were quite incompatible with the very nature of the library.

But, to the close of the nineteenth century, librarianship and documentation were largely inseparable in their development; they arose in response to the same needs, employed common basic procedures, were directed toward almost identical objectives, and in many instances were advanced by the same practitioners. The growth of archives presented a closely related problem, that of organizing a large body of documents for effective use. This problem likewise eluded solution because there had been developed no adequate techniques for the analysis of archival materials,[4] no trained personnel, and no money to finance an admittedly expensive operation. The reasons for the

[4] Archival practice did not begin to achieve professional maturity until the work of Muller, Feith, and Fruin in the Netherlands, and Hilary Jenkinson in England.

D

development of three separate groups to take care of the ob-
servedly similar processes for providing access to recorded
knowledge might well provoke an interesting study in the
dynamics of social structure. In short, one might say that in the
beginning documentation, librarianship, and archival custodianship were one. But, very early, subtle forces began to divide
those who were interested in these three activities into separate
groups which eventually became intolerant of each other.

It is not possible here to embark upon an exhaustive analysis
of these forces, but certainly one of the influences which induced
librarians to divert their energies from the increasingly difficult
problems of analysing and organizing recorded knowledge was
the new faith in the education of the masses that followed in
the wake of the Age of Enlightenment. As early as the seventeenth century the growth of mercantilism and, later, the dawn
of the industrial revolution had demonstrated the necessity for
a body of workers who were literate as well as trained in specific
manual skills. This practical need was later reinforced by the
results of the political revolutions in Britain and on the Continent
and by the establishment of a rapidly growing democracy based
on almost universal male suffrage in the United States.

Nurtured by a new awareness of the importance of the individual, a new credo of social progress, a growing belief, on
both sides of the Atlantic, that universal education held the
key to the advance and improvement of society, there arose a
group of zealous individuals who sought to bring about on
behalf of the masses a fusion of popular culture and the traditional
classical education of the upper classes. In the wave of enthusiasm for an expanded popular culture the librarians soon
became immersed. By the decade of the 1850s the public library
was becoming universally regarded as primarily an educational
agency, an instrument for the extension of the formal educational process throughout mature life. In both Britain and the
United States the library shared with the lyceum, the workers'
institute, and similar agencies designed to foster the education
of the adult, the excessively enthusiastic support of those who
held tenaciously to a faith in the capacity of the ordinary man
for self-improvement. The concept of the library as 'the crown-
ing glory of our public schools' was a powerful weapon in the
skilful hands of Henry Barnard, Horace Mann, and other leaders

who threw the weight of their influence in support of legislation for public library promotion. In Britain the growing demand for the democratization of culture made vocal by such leaders as Edward Edwards resulted in the Public Libraries Act of 1850. On the Continent the activities of the several ministries of education and the spreading enthusiasm for popular education played an important part in the establishment of popular libraries supported either by philanthropy or by public appropriation. On both sides of the Atlantic this universal urge for the extension of the privileges of education to all sectors of the population not only shaped the pattern of library development to the present day but has actually helped to drive the library away from its original course. And when, at the turn of the twentieth century, the problems of bibliographic organization became increasingly oppressive, the 'documentalists' did not turn to the librarians for either advice or leadership. By 1900 there was every indication that librarianship had largely forsaken an early concern with providing subject access to books, and that if documentation was to advance, it must seek out alone the answers to its problems. At about this time, then, the lines of development of librarianship and documentation, which previously had followed a common course, began seriously to bifurcate. The librarians went searching for a Utopia in which even the poorest man could, through the medium of the public library, make himself rich in the wisdom of the ages. The documentalists began to attack, albeit somewhat amateurishly, a few of the bibliographic problems by which they found themselves increasingly bewildered.

Documentation, as a discipline distinct from librarianship, may be said to have begun on the Continent of Europe at the close of the nineteenth century. As Bradford has shown in his *Fifty Years of Documentation*, Paul Otlet and Henri La Fontaine laid the foundation of an international movement for world documentation at their historic meeting at Otlet's home in the rue de Florence, Brussels, in 1892. From the meeting of these two men came a series of important events that shaped the progress of documentation for more than a generation. It was they who planned the Office International de Bibliographie which, after a series of changes in name, eventually became the Fédération Internationale de Documentation. It was they who conceived a universal international bibliography to which was to be attached an international reference library of subject bibliographies. And it was they who, in 1895, called the first international conference on bibliography.

Almost simultaneously with the pioneering work of Otlet and La Fontaine, the Royal Society of London began to address itself to the need for the systematization of scientific literature, a problem which had been emphasized by Joseph Henry of the Smithsonian Institution when he addressed the British Association for the Advancement of Science meeting in Glasgow in 1883. Henry's proposal for a catalogue of scientific papers was brought nearer realization when the Royal Society at its meeting in July 1896 laid the foundation for its *International Catalogue of Scientific Literature*, which began publication in 1901.

Further description of the emerging pattern of documentation at the national and international level is inappropriate to the present discussion; this subject has already been admirably treated elsewhere.[5] However, it is important to point out that as librarians increasingly became indifferent to the elements of the documentation process within their profession and grew more and more deeply involved in the democratization of education, non-librarians, and especially those interested in the organization of the literature of science, picked up the tasks of bibliographic organization at the point where the librarians had left them.

The divergence of opinion as to the proper function or objective of the library itself would not have proved so disruptive if there had been adequate recognition, at the same time, of the different nature of the collections and of the organizational machinery required to satisfy different kinds of demand. For example, a library planned for purely educational purposes operates most satisfactorily with a collection of well-chosen titles limited in number but duplicated in sufficient quantity to permit simul-

[5] See especially:

S. C. Bradford, 'Fifty Years of Documentation', Chapter VIII of his *Documentation*, 1953.

E. M. R. Ditmas, 'Co-ordination of Information; a Survey of Schemes Put Forward in the Last Fifty Years', *Journal of Documentation*, Vol. 3, no. 4 (March 1948), pp. 209–221.

Kathrine O. Murra, *History of Some Attempts to Organize Bibliography Internationally*. J. H. Shera and M. E. Egan (eds.) *Bibliographic Organization* (Chicago: University of Chicago Press, 1951), pp. 24–33.

taneous use for the purposes of group study and discussion. The number of titles should be sufficiently restricted to permit the intimate knowledge of each title by at least one member of the staff. Only thus can effective reader guidance be developed, and without such guidance no educational function on the part of the library can be assumed. It should be observed that in such a collection no single title is indispensable, i.e., a good history of English literature may be an absolute requisite, but any one of perhaps a dozen titles would serve. There is operative here a principle of *substitutability* which is completely absent when the need is for exact an exhaustive information, and the organization needed for such a collection may be of the very simplest kind.

Two trends in the modern use of graphic records have tended to create situations in which exact information must be found. The first, and, to the present, the most important, is the reporting of new scientific knowledge in the form of research monographs upon minute and precise topics. If a chemist wants to know the composition of a new synthetic fibre, only the report of the basic laboratory research will satisfy him. There is no substitute. Because of the very large number of such reports and the variety of media in which they may appear, a complex and exact bibliographic service is required in order to give adequate subject access. Such exactitude and comprehensiveness is not at all necessary in order to make effective use of an 'educational' collection. The second trend, one of increasing importance, is the reliance placed upon exact information for the successful conduct of business, industry, and government agencies. Again, if an inquirer wants statistics of the production of soya beans in China, there is no satisfactory substitute for that exact information.

This sharp differentiation between the 'educational' and the specialized library is demonstrated by the university library in which the undergraduate browsing room exemplifies the one extreme, and the stack reservoir of research materials the other. The curricular needs of the parent institution are met, to a considerable extent, by withdrawing from the general book stock those titles most frequently used in the instructional programme and placing them in a reserved book collection. Such collections usually have a minimum amount of organization through either shelf arrangement or author catalogues. Similarly, in the large municipal public library the dichotomy is apparent in the emergence of the 'popular reading room' as distinct from the subject departments in which are shelved the specialized materials essential to their respective readers.

In each case the educational function is observable as only *part* of the total function of the large general library, and the fact that the same collection and at least some of the same organizational techniques are used in common demonstrates the interdependence of the several functions.

The numerous special libraries established within the past half-century present a somewhat different picture. In its most typical form the special library, whether attached to a research group or to a business or industrial organization, is designed to provide exact information within the specific sphere of interest of the supporting organization. Acquisition policies are highly selective and the collections are frequently quite small. In such a library every available published guide or index will be provided and still a large part of the time and skill of the staff will be devoted to constructing special indexes or preparing abstracts according to the needs of the clientele. Only in a few special situations is there any educational function for these libraries to assume, and even these few are limited to training for particular activities within the organization, a supplement to in-service training. Yet these libraries satisfy every term in the definition of a library; they differ from the older and more familiar general libraries in emphasis rather than in kind. Indeed, many of the subject departments or special collections within general libraries approximate to the collection and services of a special library in the same subject field established within a private corporation, although obviously there cannot be as close co-ordination with the needs of any particular group as the private library can exhibit. In fact, Savage argues convincingly that the success of the general library depends upon the extent to which it approaches the subject departmentalization and the precision of reference service characteristic of special libraries.[6]

It is difficult to see why some of these are called special libraries, others documentation centres, and still others technical information services, when one would be hard pressed to define

[6] See Ernest A. Savage: *Special Librarianship in General Libraries and Other Papers* (London: Grafton, 1939), p. 314.

the three terms in such a way as to differentiate precisely between them. Whatever service or characteristic may be mentioned as an attribute of any one of the three types can also be shown to exist in lesser emphasis in the conventional libraries.

Only the absorption of the traditional librarian in the 'educational' function, and his implicit denial of the social dignity and significance of the information service, can account for the schism between the groups associated with different types of institutions.

So acute did this situation eventually become, and so sharply drawn were the lines of demarcation between the groups, that in 1908 the special librarians in the United States, under the leadership of John Cotton Dana, seceded from the American Library Association to form their own Special Libraries Association. Though a year later, at the Mackinac Island Conference of the older organization, Dana made a heroic effort to secure the incorporation of the new group in the ALA, his efforts were 'definitely ignored by the Executive Board'[7] of the American Library Association. The Special Libraries Association was thereafter formally incorporated as an independent organization.

In Britain the dissociation of the documentalists from the librarians is strikingly parallel with that which took place in the United States. The Hoddesdon Conference of 1924 led to the formation of the Association of Special Libraries and Information Bureaux, an organization which arose from the growing awareness by the scientists of their need for guidance to sources of specialized information. This organization exists quite independently of the Library Association. In the United States professional fragmentation was further intensified when in 1937 the American Documentation Institute emerged from the documentation work of Science Service, dating from 1926, and the Bibliofilm Service organized in 1935. During this period the term 'documentation' was interpreted mainly as the photographic reproduction, especially on microfilm, of rare or unpublished scholarly materials. In Britain these specialized interests created, in 1927, under the leadership of A. F. C. Pollard, the British Society for International Bibliography, 'to promote the study of bibliographical methods and of the classification of

[7] P. 88. Chalmers Hadley. *John Cotton Dana; a Sketch* (Chicago: American Library Association, 1943).

information, to secure international unity of bibliographical procedure and classification, and to foster the formation of comprehensive and specialist bibliographies of recorded information'.[8] However, in January 1948 this organization amalgamated with the Association of Special Libraries and Information Bureaux under the code name Aslib. This new organization assumed the responsibility for continuing the publication of the *Journal of Documentation*, the leading professional publication in this field since its establishment in 1945 by Aslib.

Although in the United States there is a certain amount of duplication in membership among the American Library Association, the Special Libraries Association, and the American Documentation Institute, the co-ordination of their activities is almost wholly neglected, and there is almost no organizational machinery for the promotion of effective liaison.* The American Library Association does have its Committee on Bibliography, a group which in the early days of the association was extremely important and powerful. The Special Libraries Association provides for a Committee on Documentation, and the American Documentation Institute began as a composite of appointed representatives of a wide variety of organizations, including the ALA and the SLA, which have a stake in improving the organization of the literature of scholarship. Despite the many common interests that should unite all of these groups, each has developed a tradition of largely independent activity. Whether the recent reorganization of the American Documentation Institute as a national society of American documentalists, based on personal memberships rather than organizational representation, will intensify or ameliorate the threat to professional unity remains to be seen. Certainly there are many in America, as in Britain, who seem quite unaware that the librarian and the documentalist are working toward the solution of a common problem.[9]

The basic unity of librarianship and documentation is further evinced in the procedures and operating techniques of the two

[8] Quoted by Ditmas, op. cit., p. 214.

[9] The Bibliographic Society of America, like its English parallel the Bibliographical Society, exists quite apart from the organizational pattern described above. Both societies are concerned primarily with descriptive bibliography, the history of printing, palaeography, and the *explication de texte* through an examination of the book as a physical entity.

---

* Still, unfortunately, true in 1965.

disciplines. In the beginning, when Otlet, La Fontaine, and their immediate followers were striving for the realization of their dream of a great international bibliographic centre, they naturally, and quite properly, turned to librarianship for their bibliographic techniques. Classification lay at the very foundation of their proposed world bibliography, and they adopted the Dewey Decimal System, a library system, which they expanded and modified in a variety of ways to meet their special requirements for intensive subject analysis. Melvil Dewey himself, when he first promoted the Decimal Classification, viewed it not only as a method for the subject arrangement of books on library shelves but as a mechanism for the organization of all varieties of recorded information: manuscript collections, correspondence, pictures, or other illustrative matter. The use of a classified catalogue and even the decision to employ the standard 12·5 cm. by 7·5 cm. card for the world inventory of literature were direct borrowings from current library practice. Finally, the world bibliography itself rested upon librarianship, for its nucleus was to be made from the printed catalogues of the great national libraries. In fact, Otlet and La Fontaine began work by mounting on cards the entries in the British Museum *Catalogue of Printed Books*.

As the discipline of documentation grew in professional stature, and the need for its services became increasingly apparent to those engaged in pure research, in industry, in business, and in government, and as the volume of informational literature grew in magnitude, it became obvious that the traditional techniques of librarianship were inadequate for these new demands. The documentalists began to explore a wide variety of new techniques for the organization and servicing of their materials. Books, in the literal sense, were no longer their main stock in trade. Their working quarters were crowded with a multiplicity of materials that deviated markedly from the traditional book format. They found themselves confronted with the need to organize and service special reports in manuscript, in typescript, in photo-offset, in photostat, in microfilm, and in microcard, Photographs, plans, charts, diagrams, and other pictorial materials deluged them. They began to feel an acute necessity for more adequate indexing and abstracting services. With the assistance of the technicians in the sciences they began to work on new methods of 'publication', and to experiment seriously with machines for the mechanical and electronic organization and sorting of these materials.

So important were these problems and so pressing the need for their solution that in many governmental agencies new offices, generally described as Technical Information Services, were created to deal with them. But there was no personnel adequately trained in this emerging discipline and staffs were necessarily recruited from a wide variety of fields mostly according to the dictates of chance and convenience.

All of these innovations took place largely outside the sphere of library activity. Though the time-honoured library techniques were breaking down in the face of an ever-increasing burden of published materials, only a relatively few librarians saw the implications of the work of the documentalists for their own problems. Nor did many of them fully realize that librarianship in the tradition of the nineteenth century was steadily becoming obsolete. The professional library associations at both the national and local levels still clung tenaciously to the old tradition of popular culture. They talked in a vague way about expanding their services, but permitted the transfer of many bibliographic operations to others. In short, they lost sight of the vision of the early library pioneers.

From even this rapid survey of the origins of documentation certain conclusions become unmistakable: (1) Until the close of the nineteenth century librarianship and documentation were essentially one. (2) When librarianship was lured into the popular cult of universal education and self-improvement, documentation, borrowing the techniques and, to a certain extent, the objectives of the earlier librarianship, ventured alone into the higher complexities of bibliographic organization. (3) Though the techniques of documentation were originally borrowed from librarianship, the documentalists elaborated, expanded, and otherwise improved the techniques for the organization, servicing, and reproduction of their materials. (4) As the documentalists became the pioneers in this emerging discipline of bibliographic organization an ever-widening gap separated them from the librarians, and in this schism both have suffered unnecessary losses.

THE SITUATION TODAY

The trends which we have observed in the development of librarianship and documentation are themselves the reflection of similar trends in society at large and in the extent of society's dependence upon print. In order to understand clearly the nature of the problems of documentalists and librarians today it is necessary to see them against the background of contemporary patterns of society's use of recorded information. Our own society, in contrast to simpler and smaller social groupings, is characterized by a high degree of specialization, by an increasing complexity of the machinery necessary to supply our physical wants, by constant action on a worldwide stage, and consequently by increased reliance upon print for information in every sphere of knowledge and action.

Anthropologists quite generally agree that an adequate definition of culture must include at least three elements: physical equipment, social organization, and scholarship, meaning by 'scholarship' the totality of verified knowledge and generally accepted beliefs. These three elements are so closely interrelated that they tend to advance or to decay together and a significant change in any one will bring about subsequent changes in the others. Close as this relationship may be, it is obvious that throughout the past the three elements have differed in the extent to which progress has depended upon recorded information. In even the simplest societies scholarship quickly exceeds the capacities of individual memory, and some form of record becomes necessary, whereas the knowledge required to maintain the physical equipment and social organization of a simple society may be easily mastered by direct observation and participation and is the common property of the entire community so that records are not required for its maintenance and transmission.

Because the records of scholarship were the first and, for a long time, the only records to be collected and organized in libraries the thinking of many librarians is still dominated by the requirements of this type of literature, and library systems of organization will follow the pattern set by the philosophic tradition which permeated the scholarship of the ancient and medieval world. Modern society, however, owes most of its rapid growth and change to the scientific tradition of inductive empirical research, which has necessitated changes in the organization of the results of such research almost as startling as the changes wrought in control over the physical environment. With respect to formal scholarship there are three major trends worth noting:

1. The success of empirical quantitative research in the natural sciences, leading to the rapid expansion of the body of verified knowledge, to the greater specificity and therefore multiplicity of the facts established, and as a necessary consequence the breaking up of the parent sciences into many sub-fields of specialization.

2. Introduction of systematic empirical research in the social sciences and the emergence during the past hundred and fifty years of the separate disciplines of economics, political science, sociology, anthropology, etc., each giving rise to its own sub-fields of specialization, and more recently a rather general shift away from the method of abstracting kinds of behaviour for separate study as economic, political or social behaviour to the study of behaviour as a whole in particular relational situations, such as race relations, industrial relations, family relations, etc. This may portend a major change in organization which will require new groupings of both data and research results.

3. Increasing recognition of the interrelationships, in terms not only of different disciplines studying different aspects of the same phenomena but also of the borrowings, application and reshufflings that have taken place in both the natural and the social sciences.

The statement was made earlier that in a simple society the physical equipment could be constructed and operated with little or no use of recorded information. The past hundred years have wrought tremendous changes in this situation, which might be summarized under two forms of literature:

1. *Technological literature*, at times growing out of advances in the fundamental sciences, but at other times produced through original technological research. As technology becomes more complex it develops its own fields of subordinate specializations, each with its own body of literature, and each with points of contact not only with other technologies but usually with one or more of the sciences.

2. *Operational literature.* Improvements in the physical equipment necessary to modern society have led to a complexity of operation which requires many recorded directions in order that the new machines may be operated and kept in working condition. This prolixity of operational or how-to-do-it literature, is exemplified at the simplest level by the many manuals the consumer receives with his purchases of household equipment, automobiles and gadgets of various kinds. At the industrial level this kind of information may be so essential that an industrial library may be required merely to maintain and to improve the operations of the plant, regardless of the research necessary to improve the product.

Finally, in the third area of culture which we have mentioned, that of social organization, there have been three important developments:

1. Growth in the size of social units. Today the internal organization of a large corporation is more complex than was that of the independent Greek city-state, and may involve more people than all the citizens of such a state. At every level there are more organizations and consequently more complex external relations among them as well as more complex internal organizations.

2. The development of such social technologies as administration, personnel management, group leadership, public relations, etc. These social technologies are similar to the physical technologies in that they have points of contact among themselves and with certain of the parent social sciences, as well as stimulating technological research in their own fields which occasionally affects research in the fundamental disciplines.

3. Expansion of the environment in which a single agent may be required to act and about which he must have quite specific information. Not only governments but also industrial and commercial concerns, and even many individuals, today have interests in many parts of the world and need to have exact and up-to-date information on many special aspects of the environment in which they operate. Much of this information is in the form of statistical data, some of it gathered by government agencies, some by trade associations or private research agencies, and some of it resulting from original field studies made for particular purposes, as in the case of market analyses of various kinds.

The results of the cultural developments which have here been outlined but briefly are many and serious. Most obvious, of course, is the tremendous increase in the *volume* of publication, accompanied by the shift in *form* from the book to the journal article and more recently the separate research report. With increasing specialization has come increasing fragmentation, not only of literature but also of the groups of individuals engaged in producing and using literature. At the same time, and at least partly because of this fragmentation, the necessity for communication among such groups has become still more essential. Technologies, both physical and social, draw not only from the results of what we call 'pure' research but also from the work of other technologists; the points of interaction have multiplied to such an extent that it is now difficult to draw a clear line of demarcation between science and technology and between one subject field and another.

The problems with which the situation as we see it today confronts both librarian and documentalist fall into five major groups: (1) those of providing physical accessibility; (2) those related to the provision of services ensuring content accessibility; (3) those deriving from the new demands being made upon classification; (4) problems of agency – who is to be responsible for each part of the process – and the provision of competent personnel; and (5) the task of stimulating research which will serve not only to disclose much-needed factual information but also to interpret the entire process of bibliographic organization as an intellectual discipline in its own right.

Physical accessibility. Of all the problems associated with librarianship and documentation those relating to physical accessibility were probably the first to be recognized. From the libraries of the ancient world to the great national libraries of modern times the physical preservation of records has been a primary objective of librarians, archivists, and documentalists. Until only the most recent times the comprehensive collecting of *all* available records was regarded as not only a legitimate but a practicable library objective. Today the rapidly increasing bulk of total graphic record effectively denies the realization of such an ideal, and the complexity of that record itself makes such concentration a wholly irrational goal.

If, then, decentralization and dispersal are to become increasingly important characteristics of the library system of the future the problems of physical accessibility will be increased rather than diminished. Already attacks upon these problems have been made from a variety of sectors: (*a*) the multiplication of union listings of library holdings; (*b*) the increasing use of photographic techniques for the reproduction of important records in sufficient quantity to satisfy reasonable demands; (*c*) experimentation in the facsimile transmission of documentary materials through an electronic network which eventually could unite a great number of widely scattered libraries; (*d*) the use of telegraphic communication to bring the resources of one library to a distant associate; (*e*) the growth of central deposit libraries for the storage of but little used materials drawn from a number of co-operating institutions; and (*f*) more or less formal agreements among libraries as to responsibility for acquisition in specified subject fields. Such solutions, and possibly others as yet unforeseen, will drastically alter the traditional pattern of library development and bring it into even closer conformity with the documentation centre of La Fontaine and Otlet's dream.

One must never forget that the corpus of recorded information is the very soil from which all the processes of documentation grew, and that the goal of every one of these processes – bibliographies, abstracting services, indices, even classification itself – is the retrieval of an individual item from among the vast number comprising this corpus of literature.

Content accessibility. Content accessibility is here used to designate the adequate provision of those devices which identify the particular bibliographic unit – book, journal article, research report, etc. – in which will be found some significant or relevant statement concerning any desired concept. It is toward the problems of content accessibility that the major attention of the librarians and documentalists from Gesner to S. C. Bradford has been directed. Yet despite this general recognition of the importance of content accessibility to effective bibliographic organization the problems which it raises are still inadequately solved. This failure is the almost inevitable product of the manner in which documentary services have been permitted to evolve. Today, as in the past, subject bibliography is still the responsibility of specialized groups, operating in professional isolation, and unmindful of all but their own immediate and often even ephemeral needs.

The first important professional group to concern itself with the subject organization of materials was that of the book-sellers, who were impelled to arrange their stocks or catalogues in such a way as to focus their appeal to potential buyers by subject emphasis. With the development of professional societies and other formalized groups of scholars whereby men with homogeneous subject interests sought to expedite the exchange among themselves of their knowledge and experience, there emerged a number of intra-group bibliographic undertakings which, though they were more or less adequate to immediate and local needs, did little to accomplish what Bradford recognizes as the final objective of documentary services – 'the efficient *application* of scientific knowledge'.

This 'application' implies inter- rather than intra-group communication of knowledge. Although Bradford himself recognized that documentation is an aspect of the more general function of librarianship, there has been a steadily growing tendency on the part of many documentation services and agencies to draw apart from this holistic concept of communication, which is implicit in librarianship. Even Bradford, though he occasionally recognized that the social sciences must participate in the documentation process, concentrated the major portion of his attention upon the communication of information within and among the natural sciences and their related technologies. Probably because of this concentration of attention he has given no explicit statement of the rôle which the social sciences must play in the success-ful application of new scientific or technological knowledge. Without general social comprehension and acceptance of such advances the social changes and readjustments which must inevitably follow in their wake are likely to engender conflict rather than to promote a calm and rational readjustment.

The bibliographic services which meet the needs of inter-group communication differ sharply from those appropriate to communication within the homogeneous group: for the former must concern themselves with the translation and inter-pretation of the final product rather than with the description and accumulation of minutiae. The bibliographic essay, which summarizes the results of recent research and points out the larger significance and potential application of these findings, is beginning to meet this need. But too frequently even these essays have been designed only for the specialist and fail to bridge the void that separates him from the layman or the specialist of another subject field. But the bibliographic essay is itself the pinnacle of the bibliographic pyramid and it cannot exist without a substantial supporting structure which brings to a point at its apex a self-sustaining framework of bibliographic communication. The absence of such an integrated structure in so many fields, rather than a failure to recognize the social importance of the bibliographic essay itself, may be the major reason for the explanation of its rarity. In an intermediate stage of development, and then only in a limited way, the abstracting service can serve the function of the bibliographic essay, but when the service becomes too large and unwieldy or when the number of small and highly specialized abstracting services becomes too great the possibility of synthesis from these sources is lost.

The other structural elements of this bibliographic pyramid are: (1) the library catalogue, which was an effective tool for subject analysis as long as the individual collection was adequate to the needs of scholarship; (2) the subject bibliography, which is free from dependence upon a single collection and which is unlimited in its adaptability to particular needs or problems; (3) the index, which is a finer screen for the analysis of book content; and finally (4) classification, which Bradford has characterized as 'the fundamental basis of the process of documentation', and which certainly is sufficiently important to merit a separate and somewhat more extensive treatment.

Classification. Though it was in the United States, through the work of Melvil Dewey, that modern bibliothecal classification gained its first widespread recognition and acceptance, it was the librarians and documentalists of Britain and the Continent who were the first to recognize its larger potentialities as a basic instrument of bibliographic organization. Conceived originally as a mechanism for the physical grouping of books upon library shelves, it could have only a limited value in revealing the internal characteristics of subject content; for a term large enough to describe the content of the book as a whole was a necessary choice. Because it dealt with physical objects arranged in rows, it could

E

not free itself from the limitation of linearity, and it did indeed approach, as Jevons has said, 'a logical absurdity'.

But classification, divorced from the book as a physical object, can become a powerful tool for the organization and analysis of recorded information in ways that make even the most minute conceptual units easily retrievable from large agglomerations of accumulated record.

The ability, first to perceive the relationship between the organization of knowledge and the systematic subject arrangement of library books; to express those relationships, refined still further to meet the needs of analysing recorded information, in terms of mathematical symbols, particularly those of symbolic logic; and finally, to apply these newly devised codes to the potentialities of mechanical and electronic sorting mechanisms promises not only a complete revolution in traditional library operations but a new era in the effective organization and analysis of graphic record.

The Universal Decimal Classification, for which Bradford was the foremost spokesman in the English-speaking world, was the first important attempt to expand the concept of a bibliothecal classification in such a way as to emphasize relationships, aspects, and points of view as well as substantive book content. S. R. Ranganathan, as an inspired pupil of Berwick Sayers, carried this principle further through the introduction of facet analysis in his Colon scheme. Entirely new approaches to the problems of organizing information have been developed by Farradane, Vickery, and others. Although philosophers, pre-eminently Alfred North Whitehead, had seen the possibilities of using symbolic logic for the development of a classification system suitable to the progress of the inductive sciences, and freed from the Aristotelian hierarchy, Bradford was certainly among the first, if not actually the first, to apply these principles to bibliographic classification.

One of the most potent arguments for the importance of classification to the international world of scholarship is the assertion that it supplies a standard medium of communication that transcends the barriers of nationality and language, and Bradford's support of the UDC has done much to strengthen its adoption as just such a standard. But such widespread acceptance of a single schematism is less important than the standardization of nomenclature, of terminology, and of conceptual units and their relationships, in order that classification may achieve its fullest contribution to the improvement of bibliographic organization.

The problems, then, which classification raises are many. The nature of the classification process itself and the contribution it can make to the effective analysis of recorded information must be more fully understood. There must be far greater experimentation in the development of specialized schematisms for specific purposes than has been produced in the past. The problems of identifying and isolating the 'thought unit' is basic to improving the classification process. Always there is the need to liberate classification from the traditional hierarchical structure with which it was endowed by the Hellenic world of scholarship, and to substitute for that stereotyped pattern the referential structure suggested by Whitehead, and to adapt that structure more effectively to the demands of modern sorting mechanisms.

Agency. Both documentation and librarianship have developed as practical arts, something that is done by someone in response to an immediate need. As the task becomes more complex, or must be performed in more different situations, critical attention becomes focused not only upon the manner in which it is being done but also upon the agents responsible for the doing. In attempting to solve the general problem of bibliographic organization, agency must be considered at three different levels: (1) particular institutions, such as libraries, documentation centres and information bureaux; (2) the various associations, learned, professional, and international, which have concerned themselves with the problems of standardization and co-ordination in this field; and (3) the individuals who staff the institutions and provide the leadership for the associations, and whose training and qualifications are really the determining factor in ultimate success or failure.

The chief problem arising from the nature of the particular institutions involved is to make certain that the totality of significant literature is collected, recorded, and preserved somewhere and is thereafter made available to serious workers who may have no immediate connection with the institution which owns the document; it is, in effect, the problem of co-ordinating physical accessibility. The age of library individualism, which covered a period of some two thousand years and may be said to have ended approximately at the close of the nineteenth century, left a heritage of legal, social, and psychological involvements which tend to perpetuate parochialism. In an age when parochialism in the communication of knowledge is no longer tolerable, both librarians and documentalists tend to think of their profession in terms of a time when libraries were few in number, their holdings small, their clientele restricted in a variety of ways to a homogeneous and limited world of scholarship, and their relationships one with another were almost nil. Growth spelt the doom of the age of individualism and destroyed, probably for ever, the medieval concept of the library. This growth was everywhere evident – growth in the volume of accumulated knowledge, growth in the bulk of record, growth in the amount and intricacy of apparatus necessary for the prosecution of research, growth in the number of people engaged in that research, growth in the number and variety of agencies concerned with this mounting demand for the prosecution of inquiry, and growth in the number and diversity of subject fields concerned. Libraries of the traditional type have set to work within the restrictive terms of their establishment and ownership to solve some of these problems through such devices as co-operative cataloguing or the distribution of printed cards, co-operative acquisition and storage plans, and inter-library loan or the reproduction of materials too rare or valuable to permit of extra-mural use. Some progress has been made toward legal establishment of centralized library services or at least in the authorization of larger units of service.

At the same time there has been a counter-movement toward separatism arising from the apparent necessity on the part of certain governmental agencies and of competitive industrial or commercial concerns to restrict the use of their library materials or even the publication of the results of their own research. Although some degree of restriction may be unavoidable at present there is great danger that the institutional pattern of separatism and secrecy will inadvertently be extended to areas where it is not at all necessary and even prejudicial to the best interests of society. It is for this reason, as well as the recognition of the impossibility of self-sufficiency today, that each particular establishment must reconsider its responsibility not only to its immediate clientele but also to society at large. The old tradition that knowledge belongs to the world must not be permitted to die by default.

The problem of co-ordinating content accessibility is probably best solved through a rational division of responsibility between the particular institutions directly concerned with documentation or library service and the associations which represent the next higher level of organization. There have been many instances of individual libraries making very valuable contributions through the publication of their own catalogues or the compilation of major bibliographies, yet it is certainly true that most of the more highly specialized bibliographic services are sponsored by professional societies. Because such enterprises are directed solely toward the membership of the sponsoring organization, sometimes with little knowledge of other facilities or needs and because they depend upon the economic resources of the group, there are many lacunae, much duplication, and little inter-group communication. International organizations such as the League of Nations and the United Nations have addressed themselves to this problem but the roots are indisputably national and there must be a thorough reconstitution of the entire bibliographic machinery of the leading nations before a true cosmopolitanism in bibliography can be achieved. At the top there must be complete national enumerative bibliography, without which no system for the dissemination of specialized information can efficiently operate; this is the minimum bibliographic responsibility of a modern national government. At the intermediate level there must be an integrated system for the subject analysis of recorded information for a wide variety of purposes and types of use; it is in this area that the intelligent division of responsibility based upon recognition of all needs of any social importance is most vital and at the same time most difficult to achieve. We need much more exact information than we now have, and the provision of this information is a professional responsibility of the first order of magnitude.

Personnel. Of all the problems of agency, those connected with the qualifications of the individuals who staff the various institutions and who do the actual work are fundamental. This is not the place to bring up again the much discussed controversy over subject training as opposed to library or documentation training.

Prior to the question of appropriate training, and far more essential, is the question of what background of knowledge and what intellectual skills are requisite not only for the successful performance of a particular job but also as the common possession of all members of the group interested in the same general objective. Although the documentation process may vary in some degree from situation to situation, there can be rational discussion of this problem only upon acceptance of the premise that such situations do have elements in common and that all contribute to a common objective which is of general social importance. That this premise is valid is manifest in the many inter-associational and inter-national attempts to standardize and co-ordinate bibliographic organization. The first task, then, of those who are genuinely concerned with either librarianship or documentation[10] as a profession is to define clearly and exactly just what the common objective is and wherein lies its social importance. Once this has been done, the next task, that of dividing the total responsibility among groups of similar agencies, should become easier. Finally, it should be possible to identify the operational elements which are common to all types of agencies and those which are common only to groups or clusters of such agencies.

The transition from what the profession as a whole must know and be able to do, to what the individual engaged in the profession must know and be able to do then becomes relatively simple. The individual must be aware of the common social objective and must be familiar with the design and operation of the machinery necessary to attain this objective, a body of knowledge for which the present authors have frequently used the phrase 'the structure and dynamics of social intelligence'. Beyond this, the individual must be equipped with the specific subject knowledge and the technical skills required for effective collection and organization of materials in his own field of specialization for, reduced to fundamentals, both documentation and librarianship are concerned with (1) the acquisition of *appropriate* materials, and (2) their organization and interpretation for effective use. The term 'appropriate' will vary in

---

[10] And although both terms are used throughout this essay it has already been made clear that the two are nearly synonymous or at the very least they are parts of the same unitary concept.

its referential elements from situation to situation depending upon the requirements of the specialization involved and it is this ability to determine appropriateness which most observably derives from subject knowledge. The possibility that the referential elements, as such, can be empirically identified, classed and taught as a generalized procedure for the approach to any subject field has not been sufficiently explored but its further exploration is the responsibility of those charged with education in this field. Recent experimentation with multi-dimensional or faceted classification constitutes one approach to such a study but it needs development from analysis of the literature and the use of literature. The organization and interpretation of materials, through bibliographies, catalogues, classification systems, abstracting and indexing services, has long been a central feature of professional education for librarianship and instruction in the characteristics and use of the standard tools has been developed with considerable success. Such instruction, however, is both static and sterile unless it is supplemented by the insights and skills needed to adapt, to improve, or to create tools for greater effectiveness or for new purposes.

From the generalizations stated above it becomes possible to identify eleven basic propositions that underlie the professional education of personnel adequately prepared to deal with the tasks of both documentation and librarianship:

1. To know what is *appropriate* for acquisition in any specific situation requires subject knowledge and this is best achieved through subject specialization.

2. Subject bibliography, but not substantive subject matter, is the province of professional education for those documentalists and librarians who are to become responsible for acquisition.

3. This subject bibliography may be adequately taught to those who have substantive knowledge in fairly broad fields of specialization, e.g., the natural sciences, the physical sciences, the social sciences, and the humanities.

4. As to organization, a standard system, like the Dewey Decimal or the UDC, may effectively be taught in a fairly routine manner so that it may be used intelligently by even the neophyte, and this kind of skill in the manipulation of a widely used system should be mandatory for all those responsible in any way for the organization of bibliographic materials.

5. But, when such a system is not appropriate to a specific situation it is the responsibility of the professional librarian or documentalist to devise new systems or adapt and modify old ones, and for this purpose he must be armed with a knowledge of existing specialized systems, an understanding of their characteristics, and an ability to criticize and evaluate them intelligently in terms of specific purposes.

6. Professional education must recognize that it is obligatory for each profession to assume responsibility for an identified social function.

7. The social function of the librarian and the documentalist is one – to provide the maximum effective use of graphic records throughout society.

8. This social objective implies an awareness of the many inter-relationships among subject fields and user groups, and the social dangers inherent in the excessive fragmentation of knowledge and the monopoly of access to information.

9. Any specific bibliographic operation is an integral part of the totality of society's bibliographic apparatus, and any local system must assume its share of responsibility for the effectiveness of the whole, for fragmentation leads to an isolation that is not only socially injurious but may even result in the eventual breakdown of our increasingly complex intellectual organization.

10. The documentalist and the librarian, therefore, need the same kind of theoretical training, based upon a mutual recognition of a unitary social responsibility.

11. Finally, it is the intellectual values which derive from this theoretical training that give it its greatest social importance, for such training is superior to apprenticeship as preparation for the librarian or documentalist only if it leads one to a firm grasp of the theory that underlies the practice.

From these propositions concerning the intellectual equipment necessary to an enlightened personnel one may distinguish the general outlines of a new curriculum for the common training of librarians and documentalists. This general outline would have three main divisions:

1. There is a hard core of detailed knowledge concerning the use of graphic communication in society and the rôle of the library and documentation services in that system whereby the

segments of a culture communicate within themselves and with each other. This discipline is dominantly historical, for only through an understanding of history can the student be made aware of the importance and of the changing nature of the social relationships of the institution he will one day serve. It will also provide him with the essential background or framework within which he may relate to the whole his own specialization. One of the important tasks of education for librarianship is to promote subject specialization without permitting a loss of the perspective which gives to such specialization its proper place within the central scheme. This can be accomplished by unceasing emphasis, through both study and teaching, upon those characteristics which are common to all bibliographic problems regardless of the subject field. Such training would promote a comprehension of the entire information process, it would clarify our understanding of what makes it work, in what respects it fails, and the reasons for such failure. It would engender a recognition of the international character of the information process, and it would supply at least an introduction to the principles of logic, semantics, and mathematics upon which the criticism and evaluation of the techniques and tools of information work, and the skills in their manipulation, are based.

2. That the student must develop skills in the techniques of professional practice has long been recognized. But these include not only the traditional library techniques of cataloguing, classification, record keeping, and administrative operations but also the rapidly accumulating specialized techniques now being developed by the documentalists and information specialists. The scholarship of a profession must bear some functional relationship to the operations of its practitioners, and librarians of the future must be equipped to meet the needs for technological advance demanded by the current problems of bibliographical analysis and organization.

3. Finally, the student must be competent in an area of subject specialization in which some segment of society has demonstrated a socially important need for special services. But this subject specialization must not be confined to substantive content alone, professional education must emphasize the structure and use of the literature of that specialization, and the characteristics and pattern of its library and bibliographic organization.

Beyond the construction of an ideal training programme lies the responsibility of the profession to provide a professional future economically and intellectually appropriate to those whose educational experience it must so carefully plan. In the past librarianship has paid too dear a price for administrative competence and bought its subject specialists far too cheaply. Able and promising young men and women cannot be induced to enter the profession or to remain long with it unless they can be given reasonable assurance that they will find there not only the promise of a decent living standard worthy of their position in society but also a rewarding intellectual experience and an outlet for their peculiar abilities commensurate with their capacities and justified by their academic preparation.

Research. The 'documentary chaos' which Bradford recognized and described so clearly, as well as the always apparent difficulties in the allocation of responsibility for different parts of the process of bibliographic organization, result from our lack of systematic and precise knowledge of the field, a deficiency which only a well-integrated programme of research can rectify.

At this relatively advanced stage in the era of scientific investigation it seems strange that specialized groups have devoted themselves to systematic study of such phenomena as the distribution and control of natural resources, of political power and the institutional structures shaped by its distribution, or of economic organization and the distribution of its product, but that there has never been any systematic attempt to study the distribution and effective utilization of intellectual resources.[11] Admittedly, many of the basic problems of definition and mensuration of such resources are still unsolved; nevertheless, librarians and documentalists have, in the records which pass daily through their hands, the tangible evidence of a very considerable part of the socially significant product of those resources. Refinement and standardization of classification systems point the way toward techniques of description and measurement which would not only be useful for retrieval but perhaps even more useful in providing statistics for a basic science or discipline.

This is not the place to sketch the skeleton of a still undeveloped basic discipline, for the authors have done this else-

[11] Margaret E. Egan and Jesse H. Shera, 'Foundations of a Theory of Bibliography', *Library Quarterly*, Vol. 22, no. 2 (April 1952), pp. 125–137.

where.[12] It is obvious, nevertheless, that research is needed at *two* levels, which might be described as 'fundamental' and 'managerial' although there is not necessarily a hard line between the two. By managerial research is meant studies of the use of literature or of bibliographic tools by specific groups, studies of coverage or lack of it, studies of characteristics of the literature, as illustrated by Bradford's analysis of the dispersal of relevant journal articles and his formulation of the 'law of scattering', etc. By fundamental research we mean the collection and analysis of evidence which will in time accumulate into a systematic body of knowledge illuminating the still unexplored problem of the structure and dynamics of social intelligence, a basic discipline which will contribute to the fuller comprehension of man in society as well as to the solution of the particular problems of graphic communication.

In all the ferment of the past few decades may be seen the roots of a new bibliographic system, conceived in unity, flexibly shaped to meet many different needs, made comprehensive through integration and synthesis rather than through monolithic bureaucracy, and firmly rooted in the understanding of the social importance of effective use of recorded knowledge. The great value of Bradford's work, seen in summary form in his slim volume of collected essays, is that he opened doors toward the solution of so many of the problems which seemed to bar the way to progress. The finest memorial to the pioneering work of S. C. Bradford would be a firm resolution to carry forward the programme which he so ably initiated.

[12] This theory has been more fully developed in the authors' essay 'Foundations of a Theory of Bibliography', op. cit.

3: *The Propaedeutic of the New Librarianship*

THE PRECOCITY of the ten-year-old Joanna, who became the legendary Pope Joan, was sufficiently astonishing that her father (or more accurately, her mother's husband) decided to exploit for his own financial gain the child's peculiar powers of information storage and retrieval. The idea came to him, you will recall, as he watched trained bears in the local festivals. He stuffed the young Joanna's brain with dogma, demonology, and Scholasticism, and invited audiences to examine the girl in any branch of human knowledge. She, 'casting her hook into the ocean of her memory, always drew up the correct answer, often supporting it with a verse from the scriptures or a text from Boniface'.

This story is presented here, not to document the observation of Erasmus that a sensible man can learn a number of useful things from a bear, or even to rub your noses in the knowledge that the first specialist in information retrieval was a woman and a child at that, but rather to emphasize that the problems with which we will be wrestling these next few days are far from being new, and that information retrieval has long been exploited for crass commercial ends. Even in the idea of mechanization there is no novelty. Lemuel Gulliver found the scientists in the grand academy of Lagado experimenting with a machine that could not only retrieve but also fabricate knowledge when properly 'programmed'. Nor was this idea original with Jonathan Swift, who drew his materials for *Gulliver* from many accounts of happenings in strange and imaginary lands.

But to return to the child Joanna and her accomplishments as

Presented before the Conference on Information Retrieval Today. University of Minnesota Library School. Minneapolis, Minnesota, September 19–22, 1962. Originally published in Wesley Simonton (ed.) *Information Retrieval Today* (Minneapolis: University of Minnesota Center for Continuation Study, 1963), pp. 5–19.

a retriever of scientific information; if the sample catechism which Royidis presents is typical, they did leave something to be desired.

> *Tell me, daughter, what is tongue?*
> *Air's whip.*
> *What is air?*
> *The element of life.*
> *What is life?*
> *For the happy a pleasure, for the poor a torture,*
> *for all an expectation of death.*
> *What is death?*
> *Exile on unknown shores,*

and so on. All of which is much too distressingly suggestive of the results of mechanized searching of the *Syntopicon* in 'Library 21' at the Seattle fair. But one must remember that the world of knowledge in Joanna's day did not offer much opportunity for originality. The dogma of Scholasticism was precise, limited in both breadth and depth, and intolerant of dissent – in short, it was dogmatic. The medieval scholar did not need a very long line to fish in the shallow ocean of the collective memory, nor very extensive bibliographic apparatus to guarantee a catch. True, the catch might not be particularly nourishing, but at least the angler was certain that his hook would bring up something – the chances of a 'false drop' were slender indeed. An IBM computer would probably have been of little use to William of Ockham or Isidore of Seville.

HISTORY OF LIBRARIES AND SCHOLARSHIP

With the exceptions of the great collections at Alexandria and Pergamum, the libraries of the Graeco-Roman world were extremely modest in size, and very little is known of the manner of their organization, probably because there is little to know. Aristotle, who bequeathed his own books to Theophrastus, is supposed to have taught the kings of Egypt how to organize a library, but no record has survived to indicate the nature or extent of that instruction. If the libraries of the Classical world were small, those of the early Christian era were infinitesimal. The typical monk, rummaging about in his chest of parchment codices, needed nothing more than his own memory and simian search to retrieve an elusive passage in support of his argument against the unbelievers. For centuries the scholarship of Christendom remained inferior to that of Greece and Rome. The Dark Ages were really dark; the flickering torch of Classical scholarship, especially in its illumination of the physical world, was passed through the Byzantine culture, and a number of others of which little is known, before it again burned brightly, this time in the world of Islam. During the twelfth century there came to Sicily, Toledo, and other centers of linguistic and cultural ferment in Moorish Spain, the great translators who made available to the newly established universities of Europe, Latin versions of the *corpus* of Classical scholarship and its Islamic laminations. By the fourteenth century all the great works of ancient learning were available to the West. Slowly, if falteringly, the soil was being prepared for the precursors of science. The Middle Ages were passing, and if the lamp of erudition was flickering, at least it was emitting some illumination. Nicole Oresme at the University of Paris, the great school of astronomers and mechanicians at Merton College, Cardinal Nicolas of Cues who insisted upon accuracy of measurement, and his contemporary, architect Leone Battista Alberti who discovered experimentally the mathematical laws of perspective; all these men were symptomatic of the transition from scholasticism to science. In such soil was nurtured the roots of Galileo's devotion to systematic experiment, Bacon's codification of the scientific method, and Newton's powerful mathematics that revolutionized man's understanding of terrestrial and celestial mechanics and laid the foundations for a new science of astronomy. The process of growth was slow, faltering, and, at the close of the fifteenth century, dangerously close to extinction; but it was given a new vitality with the effective application, if not invention, by Johann Gutenberg and his associates of the technique for casting movable types with which books could be printed rather than copied laboriously by hand.

The printing press, however, did far more than merely relieve the pressure on the scribe. It shattered for ever the boundaries of a world of learning that hitherto had been the private domain of the privileged elite. It made possible the rapid mobilization of the new learning, first by making available for republication the entire *corpus* of Classical scholarship, and subsequently by opening the doors of publication to contemporary writers. For the first time the written word could communicate pure science and its attendant technologies to an expanding and receptive audience. Science, which previously had been the product of individual scholars whose contributions were derived from the age-old learning assimilated during years of apprenticeship, became cumulative; its pace was accelerated, and the scholar found himself compelled to read new books and thus keep up with the work and thought of his contemporaries if he was to advance. The world of scholarship suddenly became an 'open' society, and it was doubtless no accident that the century and one-half that followed the invention of printing brought with it Galileo, Bacon, Gilbert, Harvey, the young Newton, and a host of lesser scholars who were influenced by the writings of these masters. The dissemination of learning throughout this world of minor scientists could well prove to be the greatest single contribution of the early printers to the advance of man's knowledge of and mastery over his physical environment. Certainly, without print the scientific journals that were inaugurated during the latter half of the seventeenth century would have been impossible, and one may doubt whether the scientific academies themselves would have survived without their journal publications. Specialization in publishing at such centers as Nuremberg and Venice was not unusual, and men began to devote serious attention to the bibliographic organization of this out-pouring of print.

THE DEVELOPMENT OF CLASSIFICATION

The change which the printing press brought to the world of books was the change from Richard De Bury to Gabriel Naudé. Only he who 'walketh without blemish shall minister to the precious volumes', wrote the good bishop in 1345, for all others, he said, 'are wholly unworthy the intercourse of books'.[1] Two centuries later, the librarian to Cardinal Mazarin wrote in his *Avis Pour Dresser une Bibliothèque*, that books exist 'for no other reason than to be serviceable as need arises'. But such utility 'is

[1] Richard De Bury, *Philobiblion* (Berkeley: University of California Press, 1948), p. 96.

impossible unless they be classified and arranged according to subject matter'. 'It is order', he said, quoting Cicero, 'that gives light
to the memory.' But Naudé would not accept the 'odd ideas' of
Lacroix du Maine, Giulio Camillo, or Jean Mabun. 'For just as,
if you press the eel too hard, he escapes your hand, so mnemonic
systems spoil and pervert the natural memory.' Rejecting all
systems 'which seem to have no other purpose than to torture
or eternally crucify the memory under the thorns of those frivo-
lous punctilios and chimerical subtleties', he accepted 'that
arrangement to be always the best which is easiest, least intricate,
most natural, most used, and which follows the subjects of . . .'
the academic disciplines.[2]

But Naudé was not the first to recognize the utility of the
academic studies as a framework for bibliographic arrangement.
Less than one hundred years after Fust and Schoeffer pulled
from their press the great *Mainz Psalter* of 1457, recorded
knowledge had grown to such an extent that Konrad Gesner set
himself to the task of compiling a universal bibliography of
world literature. In his *Bibliotheca universalis* (1545) and its
unfinished supplement the *Pandectarum*, Gesner used the structure
of the academic disciplines as a subject classification. The twenty-
one categories he divided into four major groupings: the *Sermo-
cinales* was comprised of the *trivium* of the Seven Liberal Arts
with the addition of poetica; the *Quadrivium* he termed *Mathe-
maticae*; the *Ornantes* included magic, geography, history, and
the arts; and finally, Gesner denominated *Substantiales* all
branches of philosophy from natural to political, and the three
academic faculties of law, medicine, and Christian theology.

Nineteenth- and early twentieth-century theories of bibliographic classification were the product of many hands and the
philosophical speculations of many cultures, but in the succession
of arbitrary systems fabricated for the organization of books,
there can be found no consistent growth that deserves to be
regarded as a trend, although the systems of Aristotle, Gesner,
Bacon, and Ampère did exert some influence upon the library
classifications of Callimachus, Bouillaud, Merlin, Harris, and
Dewey. Librarians, like other human beings are children of their
environment who cannot divorce themselves entirely from the

[2] Gabriel Naudé, *Advice on Establishing a Library* (Berkeley: University of
California Press, 1950), p. 65.

intellectual currents which permeate the air they breathe. But in general, practical convenience was much more influential than were theoretical considerations. Librarians have always been an intensely pragmatic breed. Thus, the pattern of organization into the Seven Liberal Arts and the university faculties of law, medicine, and theology is conspicuous in many early library schemes. Even today, modern library classification is strongly influenced by the system of the Paris booksellers as modified for library situations by Bouillaud, Martin, Guillaume de Bure, Barbier, Achard, Horne, and, most important of all, Brunet. Brunet employed five major categories: Theology, Jurisprudence, Sciences and Arts, Polite Literature, and History, with Bibliography and Polygraphy appended. The sequential parallel with Dewey and the inverted Baconian of Harris is obvious. Commentators, especially the French, have been almost lyrical in their praise of this system. On the Continent it became enormously popular for the arrangement, not only of libraries but also of bibliographies, booksellers' catalogs, and the bookstocks of bookstores. Even on this side of the Atlantic it challenged, for a brief period, the supremacy of Dewey.

There was, then, no novelty in library classification when Dewey saw his vision of the decimal system in the Amherst College chapel. Philosophically, the young Melvil was a descendant, and a not very comprehending descendant, of Bacon and Harris, but the scheme he derived from them he forced into the decimal mold. Had he not been swept away by his enthusiasm for the magic number *ten*, he might have heeded the words of Gabriel Naudé, written two and one-half centuries earlier, that discrimination among books at will 'without labor, without difficulty, and without confusion . . . could never be accomplished if we tried arranging them after a plan of a hundred cases, as Lacroix du Maine proposes'.[3] Dewey's unique contribution to library classification was not so much that he endowed it with a philosophy, as that he gave it a market value and was able to merchandise it.

Charles Ammi Cutter, who was Dewey's senior by fourteen years, sought for a system of bibliographic organization that would keep pace with the accelerated library growth of the late

[3] Gabriel Naudé, *Advice on Establishing a Library* (Berkeley: University of California Press, 1950), p. 64.

F

nineteenth century. His objective was, as he himself said, 'to prepare a scheme applicable to collections of every size, from the village library in its earliest stages to the national library with a million volumes'.[4] Thus he devised a series of classifications of increasing fineness of mesh, so that as the collection grew the library could shift to a classification with a higher discriminatory power much as an automobile shifts to a higher gear as its speed is increased. The plan was excessively contrived, and too ingenious for its own good, and it was abandoned because it failed to take into account the fact that library growth is not orthogenetic, not an unvarying constant in all subject areas. Nevertheless, Cutter, unlike Dewey, was concerned with the scholarship of bibliographic organization, and he was groping, however clumsily, toward a theory of bibliographic systematization. Martel and Hansen apparently kept Cutter's structure in mind as they sorted the books in the Library of Congress. Thus their only achievement was to reshape Cutter's outline to fit these books, and one may seriously doubt whether LC schedules would have received much attention had it not been for the general usefulness of the LC printed cards.

As Martel and Hansen built on Cutter, so the architects of the UDC built on Dewey, but their objective was to create not merely a book classification but also a system for the effective organization of recorded information in any form. Thus they not only greatly extended the discriminatory power of the *Decimal Classification* by lengthy and elaborate subdivision of categories but also introduced a variety of symbols of association by which recorded information in one document could be related to that in another. In short, they attempted to expand the dimensionality of bibliographic classification and to free it, as far as physical limitations would permit, from the linearity of the bookshelf and the filing cabinet. They may have fallen short of success because they were attempting the impossible, but there can be no doubt as to the loyalty they have inspired in their disciples.

All the workers in library classification have been touched in greater or less degree by the doctrine of organic evolution and a faith in human progress and the perfectability of man, but none so much so as James Duff Brown. Acceptance of bibliographic

[4] Charles Ammi Cutter, *Expansive Classification. Part I. The First Six Classifications* (Boston: C. A. Cutter, 1891), Introduction.

classification had been retarded in England by Jevons' condemnation of it as 'a logical absurdity', but Brown's introduction of open access stacks into the Clerkenwell Public Library forced attention upon book arrangement. Brown's *Subject Classification*, first published in 1908, the third in a series of schemes devised by him, was based on a personal theory postulated on the assumption of a serial development of human knowledge from matter and force to life, which gives rise to mind, which in turn creates record. Thus his basic sequence is: the physical sciences (matter and force), the biological, ethnological, and medical sciences (life), philosophy, religion, and the social sciences (mind) and language, literature, history, and biography (record). Brown reacted strongly against the arbitrary separation of closely related subjects, argued that every science or art springs from some definite source, and collocated the sciences with their dependent or associated technologies. Composite applications were placed with the group most closely related to them which, as he says, would accept them 'without strain'. Nevertheless, some strain was implicit in associating music with acoustics under physics and numismatics with money and banking, where it is associated with tills and cash registers.

Ranganathan, who ranks with Bliss in possessing one of the two most powerful minds ever to have addressed itself to the problems of bibliographic organization, is genealogically descended from the UDC, and derives his Colon system from an analysis of the growth of knowledge. Knowledge, he argues, is augmented in four ways: Denudation, the exposure of a new area of knowledge by erosion or divestment through research or inquiry; Dissection, the schism that occurs when a field has grown beyond the limits of optimum manipulation; Lamination, the imposition of one field or part thereof upon another; and Loose-assemblage, the association of two fields. In bibliographic classification *Denudation* results in subordinated classes or chains of classes, *Dissection* in co-ordinated classes or arrays of classes, *Lamination* in composite classes, and *Loose-assemblage* in combination classes. Like Aristotle, Ranganathan predicated five fundamental attributes possible for any statement or assertion – Time, Space, Energy or Action, Matter or Material, and Personality – and based his scheme on this understanding of the nature of knowledge and its expression. He engineered a bibliographic classification of interchangeable units which, as he says, like a Meccano set are capable of a variety of combinations to emphasize those facets or relationships appropriate to any given need. Thus, inspired by the Universal Decimal System he turned to Classical logic to anticipate semantic factoring and rôle indicators.

Henry E. Bliss is unique in being the one librarian who devoted his entire professional life almost exclusively to the study of classification in general and library classification in particular. From these long years of intensive thought he evolved a system, completed only shortly before his death, that was based upon nine principles: (1) that there exists in all nature an inherent order than can be discovered and established; (2) that a scientific and educational consensus is being achieved respecting the general configuration of that order, and that this consensus is becoming increasingly stable so that the possibility of future fundamental revision is diminishing; (3) that this order provides a rational basis for the organization of human knowledge; (4) that this order proceeds through gradation by specialty from the general to the specific; (5) that the serial dependence of this gradation is logical, developmental, and 'pedagogically correct'; (6) that this order achieves its maximum efficiency through the collocation of the greatest number of related subjects of study and thought; (7) that the utility of this order is determined by its value to thinkers and workers in all branches of knowledge; (8) that the constituent parts of this order define a coherent whole that is acceptable as the structure for a universal classification of human knowledge; and (9) that the system thus created is the essential basis for a book classification. Many of these assumptions were, of course, not original with Bliss, and some, at least, are open to question as to their validity, but certainly he must be given credit for having made a 'good college try'. Like Ranganathan, he attempted to lay a theoretical foundation for a technique that previously had been largely the result of *ad hoc* procedures.

ASPECT SYSTEMS

But however scientifically evolved, any system that seeks the physical arrangement of physical units (objects) – in other words, any document system – falls afoul of the restriction of linearity. The poly-dimensional content of books cannot be represented by a taxonomical sequence without elaborate duplication of bibliographic units; such duplication would be self-defeating in its complexity even if it were economically practicable. Therefore, aspect systems for the ordering and display of terms intended to describe the subject content of books were employed by bibliographers even before Gesner, though modern library practice rests heavily upon Cutter's rules for the dictionary catalog. In many ways these aspect systems have proved to be more efficient instruments for the retrieval of information than the document systems, and in their use human limitations have, in some degree, been overcome through the introduction of mechanical and electronic sorting devices. But an aspect is still an aspect, whether it is called a subject heading, a uniterm, or a descriptor; and however cleverly it is manipulated, it is of little value as a possible point of entry into the system if its meaning is in any way ambiguous or if it eludes the human memory.

Perhaps enough has been said to suggest that these traditional library methods, from which all of our modern innovations in information retrieval have been derived and upon which so much disapprobation has been heaped, were not the product of slovenly thinking or the work of ignorant fools. They have evolved over a long period of trial and error, and though the errors are numerous, the body of our accumulated knowledge is thoroughly sound; many contemporary self-styled information experts might be saved from fallacious reasoning could they but be persuaded to discipline themselves to its mastery. Why, then, have the efforts of the past and the gropings of the present fallen short of their objectives? The answer, I believe, is simple: the process by which the mind acquires knowledge from the graphic representation of it in symbolic form, the reaction of the human brain to the bibliographic store, in other words, the act of reading, is far more complex and less well understood than we have been supposing. Because for every literate person, particularly those of us in librarianship and associated professions, reading is a skill achieved in early childhood and practiced almost habitually, we are quite naturally prone to forget, or at least to minimize, the intricacy of the process that it involves. However, studies in neurology have shown that thinking is a process of pattern-making.

Therefore, before we can achieve any spectacular results in improving our access to recorded knowledge, we must explore thoroughly certain basic problem areas so that the pattern of organization of recorded knowledge may be brought into coincidence with the pattern of our recourse to it.

THE BRAIN AND ITS PROCESSES

An essential component of any real solution to the information problem is an understanding of the neuro-physiological processes of the human brain. In recent decades we have learned much concerning the ways in which the mind receives and manipulates information, but there are still vast areas of mental activity, dark continents of the brain, that remain to be explored. Every microsecond the nervous system bombards the brain with great quantities of information in the form of stimuli. This information it must sort – reject, preserve in the memory, analyze, compare with past experience, and in other ways process – so that decisions can be made or conclusions reached on the basis of indications and probabilities even if the facts are not always clearly understood. What, then, is the psychological foundation of judgment, and how does the acquisition, selection, storage, and retrieval of information contribute to it? Meaningful and helpful analogies between the brain and both digital and analog computers and other electronic devices have been made by von Neumann and others, and the more we work with these high-powered mechanisms, the better our understanding of the circuitry of the brain and the logical structure of the nervous system. Information theory has contributed much to our understanding of the message- or signal-carrying capacity of the nervous system, and the emerging science of bionics may be expected to contribute even more, but because our perception is still based largely upon frequency of impulses, this informational capacity is largely interpreted in mathematical, even statistical, terms. On the other hand, such scientists as von Neumann have doubted that the language of the brain is either logical or arithmetical.[5] What, then, is the character of the communication flow within the human brain, and how can we more nearly simulate it in the organization of the recorded

[5] John von Neumann, *The Computer and the Brain* (New Haven: Yale University Press, 1958), pp. 80–82.

information upon which the mind must feed? What are the neurological and psychological bases of cognition?

CREATIVITY, COMMUNICATION, AND LANGUAGE

Inevitably, consideration of the nature of thought leads to speculation about the conditions of creativity. Poincaré speaks of creativity as the making of combinations that reveal unsuspected kinship between and among facts or observations long known but wrongly believed to be strangers to each other – a placing of things in new perspective.[6] But the act of creativity is much more than selecting from the known and generating a welter of permutations, only a few of which will be fruitful. It is at this point that we must part company with the computer, for though man and machine can live harmoniously together in a profitable symbiotic relationship, creativity implies judgment, discrimination, choice; it is not algorithmic, but heuristic. Even the scientist speaks of his 'intuition' and of serendipity.

Any consideration of the process of cognition inevitably raises the question of the rôle of communication and language in that process. Susanne Langer says that language is man's greatest invention,[7] and von Neumann calls it an historical accident.[8] But whatever it is, we must confess to great ignorance about it while admitting that it permeates in a variety of subtle ways the whole intellectual process. The act of communication (whether it employs mathematics, syntax, or logic, as its vehicle) may have essential variants of which we are unaware, or it may exist in forms quite different from those with which we are familiar. Indeed, our expanding knowledge of the brain and the structure of its communication system suggests that this is so. What is the true relationship between language and reality? I submit, for example, that Ranganathan's categories of time, space, matter, etc., should be regarded as no more than pragmatic grammatical sieves to be employed as convenience and utility dictate. It may or may not be true that our concept of reality is limited and shaped by language. Certainly the utility of language is determined by

[6] Henri Poincaré, *Science and Method* (New York: Nelson, 1914), p. 78.
[7] Susanne K. Langer, *Philosophy in a New Key* (Cambridge: Harvard University Press, 1942), p. 83.
[8] von Neumann, op cit., p. 81.

the degree to which it conforms to the discovered regularities and irregularities of experience, and so to conform, it should be appropriate to the expression of everything that is, or might be, the case. Language is probably a poor mirror of reality at best and between it and experience there is no true identity. Alfred North Whitehead saw in the origins of language little more than the signal or other form of primitive expression that conveyed a reaction to an immediate situation in the environment. But whatever its origins there can be no doubt that language is a social invention without which culture by definition cannot be said to exist. But we do not yet understand its nature as a vehicle for the transmission of information symbolically represented. We do not know the effect of the symbolic structure that is language upon the behavior patterns of society. Many scholars hold that the obtuseness of language renders it almost incapable of communicating much more than the familiarities of daily life. Certainly anyone who deals with abstract or novel ideas is constantly, often painfully, reminded of the limited capacity of words to convey thought with precision and without ambiguity.

EPISTEMOLOGY

The bridge from semantics to epistemology is a natural one, for our knowledge about the nature of knowledge itself, how it is communicated through society and how it shapes a culture, is itself transmitted through a symbolic medium. But again we find our ignorance colossal. We have not studied the epistemology of our culture – the ways in which society generates new knowledge, disseminates it, and uses it to contribute to the values the society seeks. As Ernst Cassirer might put it, man lives in a symbolic world of his own collective creation that has, as one of its principal functions, the ordering and explanation of experience. Each major advance in man's understanding of natural phenomena – the overthrow of the concept of a heliocentric universe, the discovery of electricity and magnetism, the formulation of the doctrine of evolution, Freud's questioning of the rationality of man's behavior, Einstein's rejection of the traditional concepts of space and time, the creation of a mushroom-shaped cloud over Almagordo – all have influenced profoundly man's behavior as a social being. And who would dare attempt to assess at this moment the implications of Telstar for the future of communication, international affairs, or any other aspect of human relations? We have mentioned in passing the impact of the invention of printing upon social change, and there is every reason for believing that the present innovation and improvement in communications media (particularly electronic mechanisms) will have equal, if not greater, influence upon every aspect of our lives. No one knows what their future effects will be.

Richard Meier suggests cautiously that direct person-to-person communication may be expected to decline somewhat because of an hypothesized increase in indirect (machine interposed) person-to-person communication. Similarly, he foresees a possible decline in reading because of anticipated increases in man-machine and machine-machine communications.[9] Jerome S. Bruner observes that perhaps the deepest and most subtle change in man's view of himself during the last half-century has been in his concept of men as 'knowers', and he cites the change from Edison the ingenious inventor to Einstein the powerful thinker as the archtype of the scientist as hero.[10] From such excursions into the nature of the information process and its utilization by society has begun to emerge the foreshadowings of a new discipline that we have called 'social epistemology', and this, perhaps more than any other discipline, is the basic concern of those of us who are dedicated to maximizing the effectiveness of recorded knowledge for the benefit of mankind.

But the theory is of little value if it is not translated into action, and knowledge remains esoteric if it does not influence practice. Thus we are brought back to the engineering aspects of the information problem. There would seem to be no limit to the potentialities that automation can bring to the transmission, storage, and retrieval of information, and if librarians do not take this technological revolution into account they will find themselves in a sorry plight. We would not divorce ourselves from the technocrats, we only want to make certain that they do not go off half-cocked. We would not minimize the importance of technology and skill in the solution of the bibliographic problem,

[9] Richard L. Meier, 'Communications and social change', *Behavioral Science*, 1: 43–59, January 1956.
[10] Jerome S. Bruner, *On Knowing* (Cambridge: Harvard University Press, 1962), pp. 162–163.

but we would warn that a technology that has parted company from its theoretical under-pinnings not only can be a colossal nuisance but also can create serious intellectual and social mal-adjustments. Engineers are indeed very useful animals, and every society should have one in the garage, but a society of engineers only will take us back to Laputa and the Grand Academy of Lagado.

THE PEDAGOGIC PROBLEM

Finally, there is the pedagogic problem; for however sound our theory, however impeccable and valid our research, however bright and shining our technology, these will avail us nothing if they are not absorbed into the professional education of those in whose hands the future must inevitably rest. But those educational agencies most deeply concerned, the library schools, seem quite oblivious to the importance of the contributions that other disciplines could bring to their instructional programs, and as a consequence they have lived in isolation, failing to utilize the resources of the very university faculties which could most enrich education for librarianship. Perhaps the most striking characteristic of library education today is the widespread lack of enthusiasm for and interest in it. So long as this situation maintains, the responsibility for management of society's graphic records is in serious danger of passing to other hands and library education will continue to flounder in a morass of confused and undirected activity.

Neurology in both its physiological and psychological aspects, bionics, information theory, linguistics, communication, social epistemology – all of the many studies that contribute to the answering of the overriding question, 'What is a book that a man may know it, and what is a man that he may know a book?' – these comprise the propaedeutic of the new librarianship. Obviously, librarians cannot encompass all these studies without much external aid. I have long argued that librarianship is the most inter-disciplinary of all the disciplines, and that therefore it must seek help from every area of knowledge – physics, mathematics, chemistry, medicine – that can contribute to a solution of the information problem. And so long as library education continues to produce skilled practitioners who know only how to catalog or classify a book and/or where a fact can be 'looked up', it can properly be accused of taking too narrow a view of its responsibilities. But our argument here is not set forth in the hope of rescuing the professional ego of the librarians. Nor am I trying to build a case for a metaphysics of librarianship for the sake of such benefits to our professional respectability as may be expected to accrue from it. Failure to solve the information problem can present a very real threat to our culture.

This is not rhetorical exaggeration; the end is worth the laborious means to achieve it, the game is really worth the candle. I admit that this is a long and treacherous climb to which I invite you, that it leads through controversy, uncertainty, compromise, disappointment, and perhaps even despair. Worst of all, I can offer no guarantee that it will terminate in a promised land flowing with milk and honey. But the expedition is recommended by some very reliable authorities, and I am personally convinced that failure to make the trip can end in catastrophe.

The importance to science of a controlled information flow has long been recognized. As early as 1852, Joseph Henry wrote in his report as secretary of the Smithsonian Institution:

> The proper management of books, and general instruction as to their use, are matters perhaps of more importance than their accumulation in any one place. It is estimated that about twenty thousand volumes, including pamphlets, purporting to be additions to the sum of human knowledge, are published annually; and unless this mass be properly arranged, and the means furnished by which its contents may be ascertained, literature and science will be overwhelmed by their own unwieldly bulk. The pile will begin to totter under its own weight.[11]

He then commended Young's index to natural philosophy and the mechanic arts, and spoke with enthusiasm of Charles C. Jewett's plan for a national union catalog, reproduced by the stereotype process, of all the major libraries in the United States. (This praise, of course, came before the famous Henry-Jewett

[11] Smithsonian Institution. Board of Regents. *Report to the Senate and House of Representatives Showing the Operations, Expenditures, and Condition of the Institution During the Year 1851* (Washington, D.C.: A. Boyd Hamilton, 1852), p. 22 (108).

quarrel echoed through the halls of Congress.) A half-century later, Henry Adams wrote of the law of acceleration of human knowledge, that if it were 'prolonged one generation longer it would require a new social mind . . . subject to new laws'.[12]

In more recent years, many scholars have elaborated the theory of the exponential growth of scientific knowledge, and have pointed out that the accretion rate of graphic records in the fields of science is approximately twice as great as it is for any other social phenomenon or form of human activity. Moreover, this increase in recorded knowledge has resulted in an increase in specialization, so that as the amount of knowledge grows, each individual is compelled to operate in a decreasing segment of his field. No one purports to believe that these rates of increase will continue indefinitely, but they have become sufficiently alarming that there is ample reason to fear that science will eventually be smothered by its own fecundity. Thus, in *The Rock*, T. S. Eliot asked:

> *Where is the Wisdom we have lost in knowledge?*
> *Where is the knowledge we have lost in information?*

He might well have added:

> *Where is the information we have lost?*

From the depths of cynicism, Robert Oppenheimer has cried out that 'We need new knowledge like we need a hole in the head.' Derek Price sees this state of intellectual saturation as one of the diseases of science, and looking to humanism for succor, he points out that our real trouble has arisen from the fact that no one has made it his 'business to understand the general patterns and reactions of science as the economist understands the business world'.[13]

THE NEW ROLE OF THE LIBRARIAN

Here, I submit, is the new rôle of the librarian. If we define librarianship as the management of human knowledge, and I

[12] Henry Adams, *The Education of Henry Adams* (Boston: Houghton Mifflin, 1918), p. 498.

[13] Derek J. de Solla Price, *Science Since Babylon* (New Haven: Yale University Press, 1961), p. 124.

am convinced that it should be so defined, then by *management* we must mean a great deal more than the mere calendaring of graphic records so that they can conveniently be retrieved on demand. Librarians have long worried the question of whether or not their activities defined a science or an art. In the years gone by librarianship was neither, it was a craft – in the future it must be both. In its scholarship can be found the harmonizing of C. P. Snow's two cultures. In his humanistic traditions and his scientific predispositions, the librarian can well qualify himself for this new rôle in the synthesis of the total human experience, he can once again become the polyhistor of his century as were his professional ancestors at Alexandria and Pergamum.

4: *On Keeping Up with Keeping Up*

IN ONE of his more recent essays, James Thurber quotes an unidentified character as saying, 'with a distressed sigh, "So much has already been written about everything that you can't find out anything about it." '[1] In the apparent congruity of this incongruous Irish bull lies the paradox by which every research worker, and by extension the librarian, is confronted. Moreover, it was in the attempt to escape from this dilemma of poverty in the midst of intellectual abundance that the much maligned discipline of librarianship known as 'documentation', was devised. For documentation is not a mythical line of demarcation projected for the convenience of the Almighty in separating the sheep from the goats, and certainly it is not, as some would have it, a synonym for the mechanization of library or bibliographic operations. Documentation, if it is anything other than a semantic differentiation, may be regarded as a theory, a philosophy if you will, or librarianship that is dedicated to the exploration of new ways for improving the utility of recorded knowledge, for whatever purpose and at whatever level of use, by investigating and developing new means for the analysis, organization, and retrieval of graphic records. We would not go so far as does Mme Briet by asserting that animals in zoos are documentation, but we do maintain that a children's librarian can be as much of a documentalist as the most highly trained literature scientist serving the most esoteric requirements of a theoretical physicist. Documentation, then, is not a matter of degree, or even of intensity of effort, it is a credo – a professional philosophy. If the line between documentalist and librarian is difficult to draw, it is so because

[1] James Thurber, 'The New Vocabularianism', in *Lanterns and Lances* (New York: Harper, 1961), p. 120.

Originally published in *UNESCO Bulletin for Libraries*, Vol. 16 (March–April 1962), pp. 64–72.

it is not a very important line except as it has been used as a whip to urge librarians into new areas of investigation and innovation. That it has been so closely associated with science is probably to be explained by the use documentalists have made of the tools and techniques of science to achieve their intellectual goals, and because of the willingness of scientists to invest large amounts of money in the development of these new tools and techniques.

We will here, then, direct our attention to new systems for the organization of recorded knowledge to the end that we can more readily identify and disclose from the ever-swelling flood of print, that which is relevant to our particular problem, in short, we are seeking to do by means of new systems and new tools, what the reference librarian has always done, to coin a somewhat Lewis Carrollean phrase, to keep up with keeping up. The use of the term *system*, in the preceding, is particularly important, for the reference librarian, seeking to improve his services, must consider the *total* complex of processes by which recorded knowledge is generated, reproduced, retrieved, and disseminated. It is the reference librarian who is the mediator between the book and its user, and he will do his job badly if the system upon which he depends does not take into account the entire cycle by which the printed word progresses from its original graphic form to its ultimate destination in the hands of the user who needs it. Thus, to paraphrase S. R. Ranganathan, we must keep up with the world of graphic records so that every book can have its reader and every reader his book. It is the efficiency with which this cycle of graphic record to store to user operates that is the final test, and the only test, of a system's value. All this would be obvious and platitudinous were it not for the tendency in many quarters to defend a system, or a method, for its own sake rather than to evaluate it in terms of the ends to be achieved.

But before one can intelligently discuss the characteristics of any system, he must first ask himself exactly what it is that he wants the system to do, what is the universe of discourse with which he is concerned, the boundaries within which the system will be expected to operate, and its 'parameters', to use a some-what overworked term that has infiltrated the jargon of the documentalist. The characteristics of a system designed to keep the user informed of new developments as they are reported in the current literature, for example, may be quite different from those of a system designed to facilitate retrospective search. Similarly, the depth of analysis required for efficient service may vary from field of knowledge to field of knowledge and objective to objective. The discriminating power of the system will largely determine whether the result will be the provision of information in meaningful units, or merely in 'hunks' of loosely associated references. The importance of terminology and linguistics, and the rôle of classification to the success of the system are also variables that must be taken into account. Finally, the patron himself exerts or should exert an influence upon the choice of the system – who is going to use the system, and what will their purpose, or purposes be? It is the user who has the strongest claim upon the system, and if his needs are not adequately met what cares he how beautifully it may operate?

To be sure, one cannot rule out the vexing and ubiquitous question of economics, for in documentation and librarianship, as in all other forms of human activity, money does make the mare go. But one must first decide what system is best suited to his needs and leave the problem of its financing until all other conditions have been taken into account. One may eventually be compelled to tailor his suit to fit his cloth, but he should not argue from poverty, and he should compromise with his ideal only as a last resort. Above all, he must know that he is compromising, and how much he is losing in the bargain. To make do with what one has may be good Calvinistic doctrine, but history seems to tell us that it is the hungry camels of librarianship, rather than their more opulent contemporaries in other lines of dromedarian endeavor, who have experienced difficulty in getting through the needle's eye.

With these generalizations in mind, attention may now be directed to the systems themselves. These may be divided into two major groups, or perhaps three, if a combination of the two may be considered as constituting a third category. The first may be designated, for want of a better term, *document systems* – those in which the document itself, or the bibliographic representation thereof (i.e., the bibliographic unit) is the focus of the system. The other may be called *aspect systems* because the focus of attention, that which is manipulated by the system, is a concept aspect, or subject. Aspect systems deal primarily with symbolic representations of the subject content of books, or graphic records, rather than with the graphic records themselves or representations of them. The third category is, as has been indicated above, a combination of the other two – a way of escape between the horns of the dilemma when the classifier is not certain how a system should be characterized.

These new documentation systems may be most easily understood if their historical evolution is briefly reviewed, for, in general, the progression has been from the relatively simple to the complex. Certainly the system most familiar to the librarian, and probably to the layman, is the traditional library classification by which books are arranged on library shelves, in a form of taxonomic order, according to the subjects of which they treat. Melvil Dewey, who was not reluctant to take credit for initiating modern bibliographic classification, received his education at Amherst at the time when Darwin was effecting a revolution in the biological sciences. One should scarcely be surprised, therefore, that Dewey and his contemporaries turned to biological, or more precisely, taxonomic, models for the theoretical structuring and design of book classification systems. The analogy, however, between books and biological or geological specimens which could be arranged in an hierarchical pattern according to certain genus and species relationships was false. Though it was widely accepted it led inevitably to a system for pigeon-holing bibliographic units described by R. A. Fairthorne as 'marking and parking'. The logic was deceptively simple, so simple, in fact, that Jevons was led to characterize library classification as a logical absurdity.

But books do not, as do geologic specimens, have a limited number of well-defined and precise characteristics according to which they can be arranged. Rather they have an almost infinite number of characteristics, determined not only by their content but also by the ways in which they may be used, and no taxonomic pigeon-holing can reflect the great variety of characteristics that even the simplest books present. To state the limitations of book classification another way, a library may be regarded as one continuous bookshelf upon which any one book has position but not dimension. A book standing on a shelf in a library can be related to only the book to its right and the book to its left. It is a point on a line which has only position, but books have many dimensions, and any attempt to force a multi-dimensional object into a uni-dimensional system can scarcely result in anything but absurdity, be it logical or otherwise.

When Otlet and La Fontaine and their associates devised the Universal Decimal system for their projected world documentation center at Brussels, they attempted to introduce additional dimensions by the use of 'signs of association'. These were artificial, even mechanical, symbols intended to reveal or represent relationships between and among the constituent parts of the classification schedules. The system achieved a measure of success; and even today, especially on the continent of Europe, the UDC enjoys great popularity and inspires a substantial degree of reverence. It was a good try, but the relationships it could reveal were still very limited, and it resulted in extreme complications when one attempted to take full advantage of its possibilities. In fact, it can become so complex that it is quite self-defeating, and thus leads to obscurity rather than revelation.

S. R. Ranganathan, the distinguished Indian librarian and student of bibliographic theory, devised his system of book classification known as the Colon Classification which both simplified and refined the technique employed by the inventors of the UDC. He began with the analysis of the ways in which knowledge grows – denudation, dissection, lamination, and loose assemblage – and he further deduced that all knowledge can be expressed in five 'facets' – time, space, material, energy, and personality. Thus he constructed a classification system, of interchangeable parts, that made possible the relating of those facets in whatever way was appropriate to the subject and use of the documents to be so ordered. Ranganathan has undoubtedly contributed more to our understanding of bibliographic classification than any other single individual, and the results of his work, as will be shown later, have implications far beyond the simple arrangement of books on library shelves. Other variations of book classification have, of course, been attempted (at the Library of Congress, by Charles A. Cutter, James Duff Brown, Henry E. Bliss, and others) each revealing its own special theoretical orientation or principle of arrangement. All of them are document systems in that they are directed toward the physical ordering of the graphic records themselves.

Book classification was supplemented by organized listings or calendaring of bibliographic citations, specifically classified or alphabetized subject catalogs which may be regarded as fore-runners of the aspect systems. Charles A. Cutter, who is generally credited with being the father of the modern dictionary catalog, gave added dimension to the book classification system by the duplication of bibliographic entries under as many subjects, or aspects, as were appropriate to the book being cataloged.

Added dimension to the book classification was also provided by the marginal punched, or edge-notched, card. With this system the card itself is the physical unit manipulated, just as the book is the physical unit in the classification scheme. In some adaptations the card becomes the real bibliographic unit, for it is not unusual for the card to be imprinted with an abstract of the document, or even a microphotographic reproduction of the entire text itself. The aspects to which the document relates are coded and ap-propriately notched around the margins of the card. This use of coding, especially superimposed coding, has provided this system with more dimensions than are practicable with the use of the traditional dictionary or classified card catalog. But the limita-tions of the marginal punched card are serious. The number that can be conveniently sorted is sharply restricted by the time and effort required for sorting, and the patience of the user. Marginal punching, even when several rows of holes are used, provides only a small field, and friction between the cards during the sorting process can seriously impede the fall-out of desired items. Attempts to mechanize the sorting process have overcome this handicap to only a relatively small degree. That the technique has been called 'the poor man's IBM', rather succinctly characterizes both its virtues and its weaknesses.

The rising popularity of microphotography has made possible other applications of and variations on the basic document system technique – the technique of marking and parking. The early versions of the Rapid Selector, Jacques Samain's Filmorex, and other photoscopic storage devices, related to the retrieval of documents rather than the retrieval of information. They were no more than mechanical stack-boys which ferreted out biblio-graphic units that previously had been marked and parked in the bibliographic store. This is true for the IBM Walnut System which was supposed to provide random access to a bank of miniaturized documents. Even the much publicized Eastman Mini-card did not entirely free itself from the limitation of sequential research. To be sure it fragmented the microfilm roll into minute bits that could be sorted in a variety of ways, but it still remains only highly engineered and refined marking and parking. It, and Project Walnut, represent as no other devices do the error of first designing a piece of hardware and then searching for a system to exploit its capabilities. This is, indeed, putting the cart, albeit an elaborate and very expensive cart, before the horse.

The true aspect systems, as has already been indicated, derived from the subject index and subject catalog. Taube's Uniterms, for example, are no more than a form of word indexing or concordance making – the fragmentation of subject headings into verbal isolates which can be combined, or as Taube says 'co-ordinated', in a variety of ways. Thus evolved Co-ordinate Indexing – one form of concept co-ordination. In the Uniterm system all documents relating to a given aspect, or subject, are listed serially on the card for that aspect. Co-ordination is obtained by comparing the document numbers for one aspect with those for another, and the numbers common to both should relate to both subjects. For example, a document listed on both the card for DOGS and the card for DISEASES obviously treats of diseases of dogs. The fallacy of the system, apart from its oversimplification of an intellectual process that is essentially very intricate, lies in its inability to reveal the nature of the relationship between, or among, the terms 'co-ordinated'. It does not really co-ordinate terms, it merely combines them. Such co-ordination of the words John, hit, and Mary, does not indicate the direction of the action and one cannot know whether it was John who was guilty of an ungentlemanly act, or it was Mary who was unladylike. 'Noise' in the system is also generated by such reversables as *school library – library school* or ambiguities like *The Diet of Worms*. Finally, logical sum and logical product create difficulties for the co-ordinate indexing promoted by Taube. It was Dr Frank B. Rogers of the National Library of Medicine who pronounced the final verdict on Co-ordinate Indexing when he quoted the statement of Mr Potts, in *Pickwick Papers*, that he was learning about Chinese metaphysics by reading in the *Britannica*, under the letter *M* for metaphysics and *C* for China.

The Batten, or Peek-a-Boo system is simply a mechanical refinement of the above employed in some situations to expedite the tedious task of comparing the numbers on the aspect cards.

In this system, holes are punched in the card opposite those numbers which designate documents relating to the subject represented by the card. When two or more cards are super-imposed, those document numbers which 'co-ordinate' can be identified by the transmission of light, while all other remain opaque, hence the name peek-a-boo. Obviously the number of cards that can, at any one time, be conveniently and accurately compared in this way is severely limited. Mechanized co-ordination has been employed in such systems as that of the IBM Comak and devices marketed by the newly organized Jonker Business Machines Inc.

Zato-coding, developed by Calvin Mooers, represents a distinct advance over the Uniterm system. Whereas, Taube insists that Uniterms can be taken directly from the text to be indexed, Mooers made use of a standardized vocabulary the constituent terms of which he called 'Descriptors'. These, which were in reality only a form of subject heading, were identified and adopted only after a thorough study of the subject field to be indexed. Mooers also made use of random coding instead of depending upon the alphabetization of verbal isolates as Taube has done.

A variety of other systems has been, and is being, devised. Many, especially those using the standard IBM punched card or magnetic or punched paper tape, represent a combination of the document and aspect approaches. For a considerable period of time many people have been experimenting in a variety of ways with the use of IBM cards for indexing purposes. During the Second World War the Central Information Division of the Office of Strategic Services conducted primitive experiments in the use of such equipment for the indexing of large quantities of material received daily from the U.S. Office of Censorship. In February 1955 Rev. John Ellison began the preparation of a concordance to the Revised Standard Version of the *Bible*, using a Remington-Rand Univac. The task of composition, which was completed in only nine months, resulted in a work of 2,168 pages, which was published by Thomas Nelson and Sons. In Italy Father Roberto Busa has been employing IBM mechanisms for preparing a concordance to the writings of St Thomas Aquinas. The library of King County, Washington, and the New York State Library were the first agencies to prepare catalogs and bibliographies by using IBM techniques, and today a substantial amount of work is in progress at the National Library of Medicine, the Library of Congress, the Los Angeles County Public Library, the New York Public Library, the Long Island Lighting Co., of New York, and many other places where they are finding, in these techniques, new ways for reviving the utility of the book catalog which previous generations had largely discarded as obsolete. The punched paper tape typewriter, such as the Flexowriter, which has a high-speed print-out of six-hundred pages an hour has, as Calvin Mooers has pointed out, capabilities that are almost ideally adaptable to the production of book catalogs which can be revised frequently and inexpensively.

The Luhn Scanner, developed a decade or more ago by H. P. Luhn of the IBM Corporation, was an early attempt to adapt the techniques of automation to information retrieval, but his more highly refined X-794 never got farther than the drawing-boards. Recently Luhn has been promoting a method for the automatic indexing of scientific articles using, of course, IBM devices. To make possible the more rapid indexing of chemical literature Luhn has also devised the KWIC, or Key Words in Context, system, which, though it is now being marketed by the Chemical Abstracts Service as *Chemical Titles*, would appear to be a definite reversion to the old and obsolete system of uncontrolled word indexing. Nevertheless, *Biological Abstracts* has announced their intention to offer a similar service to their subscribers. For several years the U.S. Patent Office has been employing punched card equipment in an effort to solve the very difficult and complicated problems of patent searching. However, as was pointed out in the September 1960 issue of *Fortune*, it must be said that company policy at IBM has rather disregarded the potentialities of electronic applications to information retrieval.

At the School of Library Science of Western Reserve University the Documentation Center has, for the past six years, carried forward an intensive program of teaching, research, and development directed toward improving methods for information retrieval, and the Computer Department of the General Electric Co., has developed the GE-225, a high-speed general purpose computer that will fully mechanize the system devised at Western Reserve. The Western Reserve System of 'semantic factoring', makes use of a highly controlled vocabulary encoded in such a way as to indicate, not only generic relationships but also function, process, agent, product, and similar elements in the documents that comprise the bibliographic store. To accomplish this, symbols, known as rôle indicators, are employed so that, to return to an earlier illustration, there can be no possibility of accusing John of hitting Mary, when it was she who delivered the blow. It is interesting to note that, though it was developed quite independently, the basic theory of the Western Reserve approach has much in common with Ranganathan's principles of faceted classification, and the rôle indicators are quite comparable to the facet formulae.

Under the impact of so many and such diverse activities the barrier of conservatism and prejudice against these non-conventional methods for keeping man abreast of his accumulating store of recorded knowledge is steadily giving way. These unconventional methods which have here been described in the briefest of detail, have already begun to reshape the procedures of the librarian and the instructional program of the library schools. Such achievements as *New Serial Titles* and the revitalizing of the *Index Medicus* would not have been possible without the adaptation of the innovations automation has brought to library processes, and there is every reason for believing that these new winds will increase in strength as their sources are better understood and their currents and cross-currents more effectively directed.

In an important sense the title of this discussion implies an undue emphasis upon the element of acceleration that automation has made possible. The great virtue of these new information retrieval systems lies not in the speeds with which the mechanisms that many of them employ can operate. Of far greater importance is the degree to which the design of these systems compels an intensive analysis of the total problem of search strategy and the extent to which these systems can simulate the thought processes of the human being. We think, we conceptualize, in terms of patterns. It was Sir Charles Sherrington who likened the brain to 'a magic loom', and the competent reference librarian also weaves a pattern, and sometimes a very intricate pattern, in the prosecution of his search. But the pattern of the organization of graphic records does not always coincide with the configuration of our thought processes and the pattern of our recourse to the library's store. Nor can one always anticipate the patterns of future demands. Nevertheless, the degree to which all of these patterns coincide will determine the extent to which the reference librarian succeeds in his search. We can learn much from the epistemologists about the origins and nature of knowledge, and from the brain physiologists about the operation of the nervous system, and as our knowledge increases we can build better systems and machines for improving the efficiency of information retrieval. Conversely, as we work with these new machines, our understanding of the human brain should improve. There is a reciprocity here that may be expected to yield big dividends in the years ahead. No one can really tell what the future holds, but I suggest that there are at least two areas in which spectacular achievements may be anticipated. The first is in mechanized, or automated, character recognition which will make possible machines that will be able to 'read', respond to, and act upon the text that is assimilated by the machine. The second is the development of random access memories which will eliminate the necessity for sequential search, thus freeing the machine from the magnetic tape as the human reader was freed from the papyrus scroll by the parchment codex. When these two possibilities are a reality the revolution in librarianship will really have begun.

Finally, what are some of the benefits that may be expected to accrue to the small and medium-sized libraries, especially the public libraries, which cannot afford and have no access to these admittedly expensive and intricate machines? Some benefits are already becoming apparent in improved and more efficiently produced indexing services. The preparation of a concordance need no longer be regarded as the overpowering undertaking it was once thought to be. Book catalogs, with all the advantages they offer to those remote from their collections, are once again coming into their own. Not only will mechanization improve existing indexing and abstracting services, but also it will make possible the dissemination of a wide variety of current data to whomever may need it wherever he may reside. Perhaps most important of all, however, is the promise that these machines make possible the creation of a national network of information centers strategically situated so that their services, at a nominal cost, can be available to any library regardless of the limitations of its budget.

Information is a great national resource to be guarded as jealously as forests, water, and the rich top soil of the productive earth. Therefore, it must be subject to government control, not a censorship but in exactly the opposite sense, to make certain that the channels of communication are for ever kept open and free. Ever since the Federal Government established its system of depository libraries for the dissemination of public documents, man has dreamed of a national system for the diffusion of knowledge of all kinds. Through the medium of these new mechanisms, this dream is coming closer to reality. Great problems of national policy must be solved before success is achieved, but the rewards of success may well be our national survival.

Today, information retrieval is suffering the pains of growth, and the growth must be great for the pain is very acute. In this confusion of a profession in transition the vision is beclouded by claims and counter-claims set forth, often by commercial interests that have been something less than scrupulous in the extravagance of their promises. No honest person can pretend to have solved the problem of keeping up with keeping up. But for all its turmoil, ours is an exciting profession, one that has made astonishing strides in the past decade, one in which there is great hope for progress even though the outcome is not now clear. But in the midst of all this uncertainty one thing seems certain – as long as man continues to progress, and his knowledge stretches beyond horizons that are ever new, the race to keep up with keeping up will never really be won.

5: *Automation Without Fear*

THE HISTORY of librarianship, in its broadest sense, evinces the same undulating pattern of cyclical birth, decay, and rebirth, of repetition and recapitulation, that scholars have long observed as a characteristic of all historical evolution. The papyrus scroll gave way before the parchment codex, only to be reborn two thousand years later as the microfilm roll and the magnetic tape. The art of the scribe withered before the competition of sixteenth-century printers, but again came into its own in the work of William Morris and the great typographers of the late nineteenth and early twentieth centuries. Forty years ago it would have been a safe bet that the book catalog was for ever buried under a mountain of 3 by 5 cards, but modern techniques of reproduction have made the book catalog thoroughly practicable in certain types of bibliographic situations. There is even a growing tendency today to look with favor, or at least with decreasing disapproval, on the old practice of arranging books according to a system of fixed location. The classified catalog is no longer regarded as being so inferior to its dictionary counterpart as was once believed, and the antecedents of even the modern documentalist can be traced at least as far back as Cassiodorus and his rules for ordering the monastic scriptorium and library.

There are fashions, then, in librarianship as in clothes, and their virtues and idiosyncrasies are debated with equal heat, and often with as little intelligence. Perhaps it is because the librarian is at heart a missionary, perhaps it is only because he is human; but it does appear that the librarian must always oppose something – be at war with an imagined opponent, be the outstanding example of Karl Marx's doctrine that conflict is the natural state

Originally published in D. J. Foskett and Bernard I. Palmer (eds.) *Sayers Memorial Volume* (London: The Library Association, 1961), pp. 168–181. Also in *Bulletin of the American Library Association*, Vol. 55 (October 1961), pp. 787–794.

of man. But once he discovers that he cannot conquer the alleged 'enemy', he calmly joins forces with him and goes forth in search of new dragons to slay.

The present writer will not soon forget that when he was a student in the Graduate Library School at the University of Chicago, *statistics* was the main object of professional derision, and every doctoral degree given by the GLS was assumed to be the reward for nothing more than ability to punch an adding machine. Yet today librarians calmly accept statistics as an integral part of their standard operating procedure, and they no longer quail before a coefficient of correlation or the probable error of the mean. Instead, it is now the 'little black box' which is the *bête noir* of the library profession – the *diabolus ex machina* that is the recipient of professional scorn, the Pandora's chest from whence all evil swarms. One can opine that future generations, having learned to live happily with automation, will search out other scapegoats to censure.

In the vanguard of every invention, be it technological or social, there are always those who herald it as that which will lead man into a utopia flowing with milk and honey, and others who insist that it is no damn good. The application of automation to the library has had its share of both; there have even been a few who have, apparently without suffering any schizophrenic discomfort whatever, aligned themselves at one time or another with both camps – like frustrated Don Juans turned misogynists.

The present purpose, then, is to attempt to examine the application of automation to information retrieval in the library; to understand the theory that lies behind it; and to summarize as objectively as possible what it can and cannot be expected to accomplish; to the end that, to invert the famous aphorism with which Ralph R. Shaw won the hearts of the traditionalists, we may no longer flee from Frankenstein in fright. Apprehension over the advent of automation arises from three sources – the psychologic, the economic, and the technologic – which collectively interact to create a barrier between the librarian and the machine.

THE PSYCHOLOGIC

Automation is such a recent development, and its implications are so imperfectly understood, that man has not yet learned to adjust psychologically to it. The first primitive man to use a lever to move a heavy stone may have inspired awe and even terror in his fellow tribesmen, but over the millennia which have spanned the course of civilization, man has learned to accept the idea of machines which extend (in a variety of ways) his physical powers. Indeed, such inventions have come to be recognized as indices of cultural achievements. But mechanisms to extend man's *mental* powers are met with hostility, not only because of their novelty but also because they seem to do violence to man's belief that it is his mental powers that endow him with his particular quality as man. 'I think, therefore I am' has come to mean 'I think, therefore I am a human being', and that which seems mechanically to simulate thought somehow appears to rob man of this essential humanity. Thus we torture ourselves with the fabrication of robots, mechanical monsters, and mad scientists who seek the enslavement of humanity through the cogs in their cognition. This pathological fear of an uncontrolled technology is an understandable reaction in a people who may be surfeited with science, a society which has become over-committed to and placed too high a value on its technology, a culture which has emphasized one aspect of its development at the expense of others, a world that is too much action and not enough thought. Thus we make ourselves 'bewitched, bothered, and bewildered'.

In librarianship, a form of natural selection has operated to condition its practitioners against science. Traditionally, the humanities (and to a lesser degree the social sciences) have been the disciplines through which entry into the library profession has been sought. The humanist has turned to librarianship largely because he is a humanist, because of his affinity for books and reading and literature, and because this profession offers him an outlet for his particular interests. The scientist, by contrast, found ample opportunity for the gratification of *his* interests in a world which was quite ready to offer him abundant economic rewards and social prestige. Consequently, the librarian is intensely humanistic, less because of any innate antipathy for science than because of a sense of incompetence in scientific matters. Hence a certain admiration for the achievements of science can turn to distrust and fear when automation, the product of scientific accomplishment, threatens to invade the last bastion of a humanistic culture – the library.

The scientists, for their part, have done little to ameliorate the situation. From their position at the top of the academic peck order, they have looked down with disdain upon the humanists and the social scientists, and the librarians have shared in these indignities. By training, the modern scientist is conditioned toward the laboratory rather than the library; not until the proliferation of scientific knowledge forced upon him the importance of the graphic record to the successful prosecution of his research did he grudgingly acknowledge that the library may hold something of value to him.

Because the documentalists are the offspring of science and the most active promoters of automation in the library, librarians have released upon them all the fury of their distrust born of an assumed inferiority. The fact that the humanistic librarians have no need to be defensive, that their contribution to the total development of our culture is as important as that of the scientist – and in the present day perhaps even more so – does not alter the realities of the situation. So the lines of psychological conflict remain sharply drawn, and the foolish struggle continues, like the argument between the Big-endians and Little-endians of Lilliput. The documentalists charge that traditional librarians are conservative, unimaginative, tradition-bound technicians; and the librarians condemn documentalists as incompetent amateurs who proudly rediscover bibliographic techniques long since abandoned by the librarians, who conceal their incompetence behind a semantic fog of pseudo-scientific jargon in which 'reference work' magically becomes 'information retrieval'. You can pay your money and take your choice, but you will not get much of a bargain either way.

THE ECONOMIC

There are probably some librarians who fear the coming of automation because they believe that it will result in technologic unemployment. They draw a false analogy between their professional service and the automobile-supplanted horse – without thinking, perhaps, that there are fates worse than being rewarded with green pastures. A far more accurate comparison could be made with the mathematicians, who certainly have not been displaced by the great computers, but have found in them a powerful tool to extend human capabilities and raise mathematics to new levels of achievement. But the librarians who really fear technologic displacement are not numerous. The technology is still too experimental to be a serious threat to the present generation, and the increasing introduction of automated techniques into library school curricula should do much to prepare future generations for peaceful co-existence with the machine.

A far more serious economic consequence inheres in the very success of automation. Increasingly, commercial interests are finding in bibliographic automation a potentially fertile field for exploration – and exploitation. This interest is not to be regretted, of course, for it should greatly accelerate technological improvement. But such progress is bought at the price of danger from overselling. As research in documentation moves from the campus laboratory to offices on Madison Avenue, from the Government-sponsored program of inquiry to commercial drafting boards objectivity is threatened by anticipation of commercial advantage, and the free flow of knowledge and technological skill may be impeded by 'security regulations'. Few people today know, in any detail, what IBM is doing with Project *Walnut*, or General Electric with *Afcin*. That secrecy can be honestly rationalized in the interests of national security or protection of the rights of invention does not lessen its obstruction of technical advance.

A less defensible obstacle is the promoter's urge to sell. Progress in automation can be seriously jeopardized by false claims, over-simplification of problems, and the forcible introduction of equipment into situations to which it is ill-adapted. Such tactics can lead to disillusion and eventual rejection of techniques which, when properly applied, could result in substantial benefits. At the present time, most of the data respecting the economic advantage to be derived from these machines has come from those who were out to prove a case either for or against automation. The great need is for a continuing program of truly objective and reliable inquiry into the economics of automation, and such data can be obtained only through properly controlled experiments. There are probably no truly 'disinterested' parties to be found; but experiments can be designed so as to maintain a balance between or among competitors.

THE TECHNOLOGIC

It is at the level of the technologic that fear and misunderstanding of automation are most serious. That this is so may largely be attributed to general uncertainty as to what these machines are supposed to do and how they are designed to do it. At this point a distinction must be drawn between *information* retrieval and *document* retrieval, for most of the mechanisms developed up to the present time relate to the latter. They are not automated reference librarians, but robot stack-boys who, to use R. A. Fairthorne's graphic phrase, 'mark and park documents'. However, as the ability to devise increasingly elaborate *systems* for the analysis, correlation, and comparison of document content is improved, true retrieval of substantive content becomes a reality.

This emphasis on *system* is important, for it is in the system rather than in the machine that the key to information retrieval lies. One illustration should make this point clear. The great blunder in the Eastman Minicard approach arose from the fact that though its architects designed an instrument which was a true monument to the precision of the highest engineering skill, they failed to provide a system with which it could operate. Thus it sits, so to speak, in the solitude of its own magnificence like a Rolls-Royce immobilized in the lush undergrowth of the Amazon forest.

A good system will work, even with a jerry-built machine – one is doing so at Western Reserve; but the finest hardware which can come from the drafting boards cannot compensate for a faulty system. To draw an analogy: We speak casually of the 'invention of printing' when what we really mean is the invention of movable type or, to be even more precise, the invention of a technique for fabricating the matrices from which type could be cast. In information retrieval the system is the matrix which determines, or should determine, the characteristics of the machine. Just as the 'invention of printing' did not alter the basic process of human communication but only extended its boundaries, so automation gives to librarianship only a new dimension in the efficient use of recorded knowledge. Automation is the supreme example of the subservience of design to purpose – of form following function.

Here also a distinction must be made between information retrieval and reference work. This is not easily done, because the terms 'reference work' and 'reference service' have never been precisely defined. But to most librarians, either term probably implies an 'on-the-spot' check for a specific fact or, at most, a relatively small constellation of related facts, in response to a quite specific inquiry. However, this is not the kind of information retrieval for which automation is designed. No one, it is to be hoped, would be so foolish as to program a machine to ascertain the date of the Peloponnesian War, when it can be found quickly by reference to any of half a dozen books at the librarian's elbow. The exhaustive literature search, not reference work, is the object of automation. This may be a difference only in degree, but so is the distinction between a balmy summer afternoon and hell.

The real purpose of library automation is to accomplish with ease and efficiency those tasks which existing library techniques and devices (i.e., the card catalogs, the bibliographies, the indices) either cannot now do, or can do only with the greatest difficulty and inconvenience. Perhaps the capabilities of automation can be most easily understood through reference to a few sample questions which can quickly and efficiently be answered through the use of automated bibliographic routines – as has been proved repeatedly by actual tests.

First, the intensive and detailed indexing of secondary sources, such as contributions to scholarly journals, will make available ready answers to such questions as:

Where can one find references to the specific influence of Albrecht Dürer upon romantic poetry?

What are the findings of scholarship respecting the influence of the Greek romances upon the *Faerie Queene*, as revealed in studies published since Carpenter's *Reference Guide to Edmund Spenser?*

Answers to the following questions could be derived from automatically prepared concordances to primary resources:

In his notes to *The Waste Land* (line 360), T. S. Eliot asserts that the passage was stimulated by an account of Shackelton's Antarctic expeditions. What is the passage in Shackelton's writings to which Eliot refers?

What was the attitude of General Ambrose E. Burnside towards fugitive slaves, as revealed in the official records of the War of the Rebellion?[1]

Also, mechanized literature searching makes possible the retrieval of information which only partially meets the requirements of the interrogator. Here is an example of a question which requires a succession of searches in a number of types of literature, each providing only a partial answer:

In Chaucer's *Tale of Sir Thopas*, Thopas wears a helmet made of latten. Was Chaucer being humorous? Assuming that a latten helm was made in the same way that a steel helmet would have been made at that time, how effective would latten have been as compared to the steel of Chaucer's day?

Thus one is led from literary criticism to the literature of metallurgy, with respect to which two more modern problems may be cited:

Provide all possible information on the formability into sheet form of as many of the engineering alloys, both ferrous and non-ferrous, but especially high-temperature alloys, as have been tested.

Provide all information on alloys which do not rupture at a maximum pressure of 35,000 pounds per square inch, at 1500° Fahrenheit, in one hundred hours.

Such is the armor of the modern Sir Thopas!

Little imagination is required to visualize the extent of a card catalog analyzing library holdings in sufficient detail to provide easy answers to such questions as these; or the number of man-hours which would be necessary to conduct the requisite literature searches. Yet these examples have been selected not because they are complex, but precisely for the opposite reason: from the standpoint of the machine, they are child's play.

But perhaps no attribute of automation has been so widely misunderstood or so seriously over-emphasized as that of speed. The spinning drum and the swiftly moving tape exert a mesmerizing power which is difficult to withstand. Admittedly, the ability

---

[1] This problem has been nicely analyzed by John L. Melton in 'Principles of Machine and System Design with Special Reference to the Indexing and Analysis of Historical Literature' (with J. W. Perry), *American Documentation*, Vol. 10 (October 1959), pp. 278–285.

to scan thousands of lines of text in a minute fraction of the time required for reading by a human being is a very useful, very important, asset; but it is by no means the *raison d'être* of these machines. Moreover, undue emphasis upon speed has resulted in certain aberrations such as, for example, the belief often expressed that library machines are a snare and a delusion because even the best of them would require x number of hours (or days or weeks or months) to search all of the books in the Library of Congress. Now, who could possibly *want* to search all the books in the Library of Congress? And for what?

The librarians' automobile analogy is appropriate here. No one will deny that speed can be, and often is, a very useful property in a motor-car, or that under certain circumstances it can mean the difference between life and death. But we do not invest our savings in cars merely in order to propel ourselves through space in the minimum amount of time; if we did, we would all be driving stripped-down chassis with Offenhauser engines. But speed is associated with, and even sometimes a by-product of, certain other desirable characteristics – power, maneuverability, acceleration – so we often get more speed in an automobile than we need, want, or even should have. And similarly, there is more in data-processing machines, Horatio, than the speeds at which they operate – their power to conduct generic searches, to relate and correlate information from a variety of disciplines in a multiplicity of ways, to retain vast quantities of data in their memories, to search without forgetting or overlooking a likely source, to conduct simultaneously a number of independent, related, or unrelated searches, and to analyze and manipulate great masses of minute detail far beyond the capabilities of any of the traditional bibliographic media. And all of these attributes will improve as the technology develops; thus does the 'rapid selector' yield to the 'Analyzer', the 'correlator', and the 'synthesizer'.

CAN MACHINES THINK?

The persistent argument about whether or not machines can think[2] ends in futility because of our great confusion over the

[2] This problem was debated at a recent conference of logicians, philosophers, and psychologists at New York University. See Sidney Hook, *Dimensions of Mind* (New York: University Press, 1960).

meaning of the verb 'to think'. Certainly these inanimate mechanisms are not restricted, as it was once assumed they were, to a limited variety of repetitive operations, and they can at least simulate certain intellectual processes. They can appear to make decisions and exercise a degree of judgment. Computers have been designed to play an acceptable game of chess or checkers, prove theorems, and solve intricate problems in strategy. Yet the 'intelligence' implied by such capabilities is somehow unconvincing in its elusive un-natural quality – like music composed in the style of Bach by automation. These machines are sharply distinguished from intelligent living organisms by being ill-equipped to select from their environment the things or relations that they are going to think *about*. They do not have cognative skill, a capacity for knowledge, any awareness that they know.

A child begins to analyze his environment into meaningful patterns long before he can prove a theorem in geometry, long before he has any notion that there is such a body of knowledge as geometry. The computer, by contrast, can prove a geometric theorem with ease; but because it has no 'perception' other than that with which it is stored – given to it by some external agent – the machine cannot relate itself to its environment. Its environment, so to speak, is totally within itself. Not only does it *do* only what it is told – it also *knows* only what it is told. It is possible to increase the 'thinking power' of a machine by feeding back into it the human evaluations of its search results, so that in subsequent searches it can exercise 'judgment' with regard to the probable worth of alternate possibilities. But it cannot observe its external environment for itself, or relate its little store of knowledge thereto – thus it cannot grow. However, it is important to remember that except for the ability to recognize pattern, which lies at the heart of the perceptive power, these machines can now meet most of the classical criteria of intelligence. They may not be perceptive but what they do know they know very thoroughly indeed; so thoroughly that, in their limited areas of capability, they can out-perform the human being.

But whether or not machines will be made that *can* think, there can be no doubt that the more nearly perfect is our understanding of the human thought process, and of the dynamics of the human brain in particular, the better we will be able to design systems, and devices to mechanize them, for improving information retrieval. Cognition is now generally regarded as pattern recognition and pattern fabrication by the loom that is the human brain. Library search, then, is to be understood as a process by which the pattern of the searcher is matched against the pattern of organization of the library, and success in the search is determined by the degree of coincidence of these two patterns. Serendipity, of which so much is heard among reference librarians, may be regarded as a kind of short-circuit by means of which patterns and relationships not previously perceived suddenly become apparent. But how this seemingly spontaneous perception of pattern takes place we do not yet know; the secret may be buried somewhere in the dark continents of the subconscious areas of the brain. Everyone is familiar with the unintelligible nonsense rhymes of childhood, of which *Mairzey Doats* (because of its revival in the early 1940s) is probably the best known. Another example is:

In mudelis;
In pinetaris;
In claynonis;
In oaknonis.[3]

How the brain, even after prolonged contemplation, brings order and meaning out of this apparent gibberish is still a mystery. One can doubt whether, in this case, the search for pattern is worth the effort in terms of 'information' gained. But if the *process* of pattern recognition were understood, there is good reason to assume that a great light would be shed on the information retrieval problem. Or, to state the problem another way, if the action of the subject catalog on the human brain were better understood, better subject catalogs could be built, and better systems and machines could be designed to take their place. 'What is a number that a man may know it, and what is a man that he may know a number?' If the epistemologists could but answer that question, the library problem would be solved.

THE RIGHT TO BE SKEPTICAL

But if the librarian is waiting for the findings of the neurologist and the epistemologist, he will not have long to wait. Each day

[3] In mud eel is; in pine tar is; in clay none is; in oak none is.

brings us closer to an understanding of human mental processes, man's power to learn, and the total communication system. Through the work that has been done (and is being done) by such men as Sir Charles Sherrington, W. Grey Walter, John von Neumann, Claude Shannon, Ernst Cassirer, and Warren McCulloch, to name but a few, we are moving ever closer to an appreciation of the epistemological foundations of our culture. The automation of intellectual tasks lies not in some far-off future; it is here, now.

The disciplines upon which automation is founded are not customarily thought of as being relevant to librarianship. But I submit that anything which touches in any way the communication of knowledge has meaning for the librarian, and that to ignore any facet of the communication process would be a form of professional irresponsibility and, perhaps, even suicide. This is not to say that the librarian has no right to be skeptical of every innovation; on the contrary, it is his obligation. Few advances in scholarship, in science, achieve acceptance without a struggle for survival. The road to success is strewn with obstacles and littered with failures. Such is the prodigality of the inventive mind; and this is as it should be. Only thus can a culture winnow the wheat from the chaff. Librarians are quite right in demanding that automation prove itself; I merely warn that the proof is inevitable – that it is becoming more certain with each passing day, and that librarians must not erect barriers against it, but prepare themselves to exploit it for their own great, very great, professional advantage. For automation comes to the librarian not as an enemy to be feared, but as an ally to be welcomed.

The librarian, like Shelley's West Wind, is both 'destroyer and preserver'; or to use Grayson Kirk's phrase, 'critic and architect'. Preserver he has always been; it is in the rôle of destroyer that he feels less secure. 'To serve society is a noble calling,' say the librarians; but society must constantly change, reshape itself, struggle with new problems. 'Here below to live is to change,' wrote Cardinal Newman, and that which once served society may no longer be useful. In a world of mingled menace and promise, the winds of change blow as surely through the library stacks as they do through the corridors of the United Nations or the chambers at No. 10 Downing Street. The librarian, therefore, *must* be both critic and architect – destroyer of that which is obsolete and builder of his own future. If he is not, his responsibilities, the opportunity to serve society in which he takes so much pride, will pass to other more competent hands. More than half a century ago, when he received a request to pose for a cinematograph, Count Leo Tolstoi told his daughter:

> You will see that this little clicking contraption with the revolving handle will make a revolution in our life – in the life of writers. It is a direct attack upon the old methods of literary art. We shall have to adapt ourselves to the shadowy screen and the cold machine. A new form of writing will be necessary. I have thought of that and I can fell what is coming. But I rather like it. . . . Drr! and a scene is ready! Drr! and we have another! We have the sea, the coast, the city, the palace – and in the palace there is tragedy. (There is always tragedy in palaces, as we see in Shakespeare.)
>
> I am seriously thinking of writing a play for the screen.[4]

By contrast, less than a quarter of a century ago the present writer made sport of the late Frederick Keppel for his anticipation of a fully automated library, and today the Keppel dream is virtually a reality.[5]

We must see the little black box as adding a new dimension to librarianship, just as Tolstoi saw it adding a new dimension to the genius of the novelist. Librarians, too, must learn to adapt themselves to 'the cold machine' and devise for it 'a new form of writing' which will make possible the fullest use of its capabilities. Eventually they, too, may discover that they 'rather like it'.

They must not fear subservience to the genie of the machine. What man can design and fabricate, man can control. The notion that something evolved from man's technology can become greater than man himself somehow does violence to an intellectual second law of thermodynamics – conservation of intellectual energy. Machines will master us only if we place a greater importance on technology than upon the intellect. The little black box is no monster created by a Frankenstein; it is but a tool which does only what we do with it. It is only a little black box, Esmeralda; you have nothing to fear but fear itself.

[4] 'The Soviet Cinema', *Times Literary Supplement* (August 26, 1960), p. 537.
[5] J. H. Shera, 'Tomorrow and Tomorrow and Tomorrow', *Bulletin of the American Library Association*, Vol. 33 (April 1939), p. 249.

6: *Developments in Machine Literature Searching*

'HOW MUCH research for a dollar?' was the rhetorical question that Dael Wolfle propounded to the readers of *Science* for August 26, 1960. His query was prompted by the discovery that the United States, in investing thirteen billion dollars for research during that year, was obtaining a decreasing volume of research for an increase in financial investment. To be specific, his calculations revealed that, if 1950 were used as a base, more than four times the expenditure was required in 1960 to double the volume of research. Doubtless there are a number of reasons why the efficiency of research productivity should be declining so sharply, but certainly one of the most important is the inadequate availability, and hence ineffective utilization, of recorded scientific information. L. H. Flett has estimated that because of this information lag, 45 per cent of the research dollar is wasted. This loss, which is not a constant but is steadily increasing, has now reached the point at which at least one company believes it more economical to repeat an experiment if it costs less than $100,000, than to incur the expense of a thorough literature search. In the field of chemistry alone the volume of recorded information has doubled every eight years, and the total amount of research output of all scientific fields since the close of the Second World War now exceeds that produced in this country from 1776 to 1945. In an article in the *Journal of the Franklin Institute*, it has been estimated that during every sixty seconds of the twenty-four-hour day more than two thousand pages of text are published throughout the world. Hence, if an individual

Presented before the Symposium on the Clarification, Unification, and Integration of Information Storage and Retrieval (New York, 1961). Originally published in *Proceedings of the Symposium*, ed. by Edward A. Tomoski and others (New York: Management Dynamics, Inc., 1961), pp. 23–34.

with an average reading speed (but one should hasten to add, with a sub-normal intelligence) were foolish enough to attempt to read this entire output, even though he devoted the entire twenty-four hours of the day to his reading, he would fall behind some billion pages a year. Such estimates are so astronomical that they stagger the imagination, but they do serve to emphasize the magnitude of the problem of communication faced by scientists, engineers, and other professional people, including administrators, planners, and government officials. The more information our society generates the more it is dependent upon efficient access to it, this is the vicious circle that confronts us today.

More than a decade ago it became apparent to a few individuals that traditional library and indexing methods could not long be expected to master this flood of print, and the outpouring from the printing press in the decade of the fifties has more than substantiated, it has dramatized, their prognostications.

Scientists and others thus threatened with inundation attempted to save themselves in three ways: first, by increasing the selectivity of their reading and relying on their own judgment to choose the one page in a million that might yield the highest probability of intellectual or informational return; secondly, by depending increasingly upon traditional indexing and abstracting services to compress the volume of material to manageable proportions; and thirdly, by fabricating local and highly specialized information files designed to meet specific needs. But selectivity was frustrated by the increasing scattering of materials over a wide, and often heterogeneous, variety of publication media. Reliance on abstracting and indexing media was threatened by the great proliferation of specialized services, any number of which might be relevant to a particular undertaking, and the inadequacy of the services themselves in their attempts at comprehensiveness and dependence upon specialized local files only transferred the problem from the individual to the small group, magnified its economic costs, and intensified duplication of effort. Thus it became apparent that a system, or systems, must be developed to increase the efficiency of information retrieval by making possible: (*a*) the *analysis* of graphic records from a variety of independent points of view; (*b*) the *independent recording* of each individual point of view; and (*c*) the *identification* of recorded information from a single point of view or a combination of related points of view as derived from an analysis of the structure and uses of the literature and the questions or problems presented to the system. Therefore, any system for the retrieval of information must be examined in terms of the depth of analysis of the materials to which it is applied and the questions presented to it, the rôle of linguistics in its effective operation, its functional capabilities in terms of its economic boundaries, and the tools, or mechanisms, required for its successful operation.

The emergence of automation, the early experiments with computers, and subsequently, the development of so-called 'giant brains', encourage some consideration of the use of these mechanisms for improving the efficiency of information retrieval. Indeed, the present writer began to ponder this problem as early as 1938, and, during the Second World War, conducted some crude experiments in the use of computing equipment for the indexing of intelligence materials in the Central Information Division of the Office of Strategic Services.

Because of our belief that automation would have an important influence upon the future of librarianship, and hence upon library education, the Center for Documentation and Communication Research was established at the School of Library Science at Western Reserve University in the spring of 1955, to develop a program of research and instruction in the non-conventional approaches to the solution of library and bibliographic problems.

The objectives of the Center have been: (*a*) to develop a research program in the formulation and application of methods and the design of equipment and techniques that would improve the communication and utilization of recorded knowledge, and (*b*) to instruct graduate students in this rapidly emerging branch of librarianship. Thus the Center has been charged with a four-fold responsibility in education, research, liaison, and operational experimentation. Specifically, its program may be expressed in terms of eight major areas of activity: (1) theoretical and basic research; (2) investigations of user needs; (3) systems development; (4) equipment design and construction; (5) pilot, or laboratory operations; (6) service operations; (7) mechanical translation; and (8) education, including formal classroom instruction; conferences, and liaison activities with other organizations working in the field. Inasmuch as the present discussion is to be addressed mainly to systems development and equipment, the other six areas will be dealt with briefly first.

(1) *Theoretical and basic research.* Basic research is fundamental to all the other activities of the Center, and without it the total program cannot be said to have a solid or realistic foundation. With the support of the Office of Scientific Research of the U.S. Air Force, an extensive inquiry into the mathematical foundations of documentation theory and search strategy is in progress. This inquiry should lead to the formulation of valid and reliable procedures to simulate the performance of a variety of information retrieval systems and make possible the comparison of their effectiveness. Other basic studies include: the development of a common machine language designed to permit the utilization of graphic records processes for any retrieval system, without the need for reanalysis of source documents; an investigation of the language of abstracts and its mechanical translation into machine language; and an inquiry into the utility of a semantic code as an intermediate language in translating mechanically from one language to another.

(2) *Investigations of user needs.* Closely allied to the program of basic research is the investigation of user needs. Largely with support from the National Science Foundation studies are in progress respecting the requirements of users of scientific literature. Surveys have also been conducted relative to the practicability of both centralized and co-operative services in meeting the demands of both scientists and administrators for recorded information.

At this point, may I omit for the moment items (3) and (4) and consider briefly the remaining aspects of the Western Reserve program?

(5) *Pilot, or laboratory operations.* Shortly after the establishment of the Center, a five-year pilot program sponsored by the American Society for Metals to test the feasibility of mechanized literature searching was inaugurated. Accordingly, some 20,000 important metallurgical documents, of current interest, were abstracted using the Center's telegraphic technique. These abstracts were encoded for searching on a mechanical machine, using telephone relays and Flexowriter eight-channel paper tape. This experimental machine was built by the staff of the Center. After eighteen months the program was ready for its initial

test, and members of ASM were invited to submit test questions for search. All results were carefully reviewed by both the agency submitting the questions and officials in the ASM itself. Similar pilot tests were made on articles of general metallurgical interest published in *The New York Times* to check the practicability of the technique for non-technical information. Other tests were made using ordnance reports for the Proof Services of Aberdeen Proving Ground and for the preparation of a glossary of ordnance terminology for the Ordnance Engineering Design Handbook Office at Duke University. A program sponsored by the American Diabetes Association makes use of the system for the analysis of diabetes literature. Another program, relating to disease vector control literature and sponsored by the Communicable Disease Center at Atlanta, Georgia is also in progress. The use of the IBM 709 as the mechanical medium for the system is being tested at the Applied Research Laboratory of the University of Arizona using the analysis of electrical engineering report literature, and sponsored by the Fort Huachuca Signal Corps installation. Less ambitious studies are under way for legal literature (Uniform Commercial Code of Ohio) with the co-operation of the School of Law at Western Reserve, and for selected aspects of the literature of American history, education, and even musical and other phonographic recordings. Enough has been said, perhaps, to indicate that the Center's methods are now under critical test in a wide variety of disparate and unrelated fields.

(6) *Service operations.* The success of the pilot operations in metallurgy has prompted the American Society for Metals to inaugurate a comprehensive literature searching service, both current and retrospective, on a commercial contract basis using the resources of the Center and its General Electric 225 computer-analyzer, which greatly extends the services the Center can provide. This service is substantially enriched by a generous grant from the National Science Foundation which makes possible extended coverage of the literature in scientific fields related but marginal to metallurgy. A total of 50,000 documents have been encoded and are now on tape. The NSF grant also provides for further evaluation of the system by a special committee appointed by the National Academy of Sciences/National Research Council.

(7) *Mechanical translation.* Mechanical translation has been a

peripheral concern of the Center. In association with the development of the semantic code there has been some exploration of the linguistic problems involved in literature analysis and retrieval and of the possibilities of employing the code as a linguistic bridge between two languages. An international conference held in Cleveland in September 1959 brought together a variety of scholars from some fourteen countries, many of whom were concerned with the possibilities of mechanical translation. The proceedings of this conference are now published in two volumes by Interscience Publishers of New York, as *Information Retrieval and Machine Translation*, edited by Allen Kent.

(8) *Education.* The educational program of the Center has probably been least publicized, though of all the activities of the Center it is probably the most important for the future. The School of Library Science at Western Reserve has pioneered the introduction of non-conventional library techniques, specifically those of documentation and special librarianship, into the traditional library school curriculum. Helen Focke of the faculty of Western Reserve presented the first course in documentation to be offered in any library school, and Rose Vormelker was second only to Linda Morley in developing a course for special librarians. Today the School offers an extensive program for the training of documentalists and special librarians. The senior staff of the Center are members of the faculty of the School, and offer courses in mechanized literature searching, applications of computers to library problems and methods, specialized information centers, language engineering, and related subjects. Employment at the Center provides the students in the School with the opportunity to enrich their classroom studies with a substantial amount of practical experience, and advanced graduate students find in the several programs of the Center a rich and varied field for their own individual research. One should emphasize, however, that all students in the documentation program are expected to begin their studies with a thorough foundation in the fundamental disciplines of librarianship. The School and its Center have also offered a continuing program of conferences, workshops, and special seminars, and the resources of the School are augmented by visiting specialists who come to it from other countries as well as the United States to pursue their special investigations and lecture in the School. All of these

formal educational activities are augmented by a continuing flow of scholarly publication. The educational objective of the School, therefore, is not to indoctrinate the student with any particular philosophy or technique but to develop in him a flexibility of mind which, based upon a solid foundation of bibliothecal theory and practice, should enable him to adjust to whatever demands the future of his profession may impose.

Now let me turn to items (3) and (4), which may be considered together.

(3) and (4) *Systems development and equipment design.* The Western Reserve system and the electronic devices designed to effect its operation have been developed to provide a degree of flexibility, a measure of control, and a minuteness of detail of analysis and inter-correlation that is impracticable with traditional library methods and other information systems. The semantic code makes possible a wide use of terms, including synonyms, with almost unlimited provision for generic and inter-disciplinary relationships. The first step in preparing the bibliographic store involves the preparation of a 'telegraphic style' abstract which presents in tabular form the content of the original showing, for example, the substances, properties, processes, conditions, and similar components set forth by the author of the document. Abstractors with a wide variety of professional skills and linguistic competence, and trained in this specialized procedure, are employed for this task. Clerical workers then transfer each term in the telegraphic abstract to its own punched card, showing at the same time, the reference number of the abstract and the numerical sequence of the term in the abstract, the latter to permit mechanical reassembly of the cards in their original, or textual, order. The total volume of cards for each day's work are mechanically arranged in alphabetical sequence, and each term is compared with the terms in the semantic code dictionary which is also on punched cards. Cards which display any variation, i.e., mis-spellings, errors in punching, terms new to the dictionary, variant meanings, etc., are mechanically rejected for human inspection and correction. This process of comparison also involves automatic punching, on each card of the semantic code symbol for the term represented. Cards are then mechanically reassembled according to abstract number and sequence within each abstract, and the abstract number and the coded words

representing its intellectual content are automatically transferred from card to magnetic tape. Thus, the resulting product is a magnetic tape library containing a detailed analysis of the documents expressed in semantic code. Questions to be searched receive the same treatment, and the searching machine is programmed using the same symbolic representations. The search process itself is, therefore, a mechanical matching of question against the information store. Matches trigger a print-out which reproduces the document number of the relevant abstract and the number of the question to which it is pertinent. Questions for recurrent (i.e., 'current awareness') searches are stored in an external memory for repeated searching. Sub-files may also be mechanically generated to avoid the necessity for repeated searching of the entire tape library in subject areas where it is possible to predict future interest. The system, and the GE-225 also make possible the use of a random access memory whenever such a procedure is indicated.

As suggested above, the original mechanism built at Western Reserve employed a network of mechanical relays, triggered by eight-channel punched paper tape, with a flexowriter output. The GE-225, which is a general purpose stored program computer, has special routines for meeting the specific requirements of bibliographic searching, with a running speed to permit the scanning of 50,000–100,000 abstracts per hour. It is possible to conduct as many as fifty completely independent searches simultaneously, the number depending on the complexity of the questions.

The computer has an 8,192-word core memory, and two magnetic tape units. The input may be in punched cards and the output may be typed out/or punched into cards.

This equipment was chosen after much investigation and after a false start in attempting to obtain a wired program computer, the GE-250. However, after determining costs and search speeds, it was decided that during the present stage of computer technology the GE-225 would serve information retrieval needs at lower cost and greater effectiveness than the projected GE-250.

Finally, a word should be added about the human resources of our program, for, contrary to current opinion, automation does not make the human being obsolete. Beginning with a staff of two and a secretary in 1955, the Center now employs thirty-five full-time, and eighty part-time people, who conduct the research, developmental, and operational activities outlined above. This branch of the School of Library Science is responsible to Allen Kent, the Associate Director of the Center, who joined the faculty of the School when the Center was established*. To this task he brought a rich and varied background in documentation research first at the Massachusetts Institute of Technology, and subsequently at the Battelle Memorial Institute, supplemented by experience as a consultant to governmental agencies and industrial organizations. Mrs Jessica Melton, Assistant Director for Technical Operations, has played a major rôle in the research program almost from the inauguration of the Center. Alan Rees, who was educated in England and received his professional training at the Western Reserve Library School, directs the acquisitions, analysis, and reference services. LaVahn Overmeyer, who came to the Center from the faculty of the School of Business at Western Reserve supervises all support operations, including supervision of budgets and accounts. Jack Belzer, was recruited from Battelle and Ohio State University, where he directed their computer installation. A number of years ago he established one of the earliest computer laboratories for Dr Eckert at the Naval Observatory in Washington.

The work of the permanent staff is supplemented by that of Dr Jacobus Verhoeff, a mathematician from the Netherlands who has been engaged in the application of mathematics to documentation theory. His work was augmented by that of R. A. Fairthorne who came to the Center on leave from the British Royal Aircraft Establishment. Other visiting staff are scheduled for the future. The Center also maintains an advisory board composed of some twenty leaders from the fields of physics, medicine, law, linguistics, aeronautics, engineering, and publishing, and selected from England, India, Netherlands, West Germany, and other countries, as well as the United States. This group is not a façade but a working organization that contributes actively to the Center's program.

The mechanization of information storage and retrieval has much to contribute to the solution of the library problem, but with it comes the danger of a blind and indiscriminate onrush

---

*Prof Kent is now Director of the Knowledge Availability Systems Center at the University of Pittsburgh.

toward over-simplified solutions and promises of panaceas. The over-selling of an idea when it is still in its experimental stage will lead to sketchy and ill-defined programs, the prostitution of ideals, and a sacrifice of quality to the end that mechanization *per se* may be discredited and condemned for faults that are not inherent in it. Because a particular literature searching device may be shown to work well in a highly restricted and sharply circumscribed pilot operation, the undiscriminating may see in it the solution to all bibliographic problems, and a tentative proposal may become a fad in an incredibly short time. We at Western Reserve are convinced that many library search operations can be successfully automated, but we must proceed slowly and ask the right questions at every turn. In what types of bibliographic situations does mechanization seem to promise the most effective results? What refinements in search strategy are necessary to make automation successful? In an innovation that breaks so radically as does this with library traditions, what are the older values that must be preserved? Specifically, what *is* the importance of the human factor in librarianship and in the librarian–patron relation? These are questions that will not be answered overnight or by a hasty polling of opinion. Nor will they be answered by any one group of individuals or at any one school. Here are problems that challenge *all* the intellectual resources that can be brought to bear upon them.

Some ten years ago we heard Enrico Fermi assert that the farther man probed into the interior of the atom, the farther Nature seemed to keep ahead of him. Much the same can be said for our explorations into the problem of information retrieval, for the relationship between reader and book, between literature searcher and literature searched, is far more complex and subtle than has been supposed. In this matching of pattern of recourse to graphic records with the pattern of their content and organization there can be no short-cuts, no easy solutions. Certainly we do not pretend to have solved the information retrieval problem at Western Reserve. But if we have learned anything from our investigations it is that one cannot begin with hardware, with a machine, and work backward to the solution of the problem. America's peculiar genius for engineering has led us into snarls that are only too apparent in our urban traffic congestion. Information retrieval, too, can suffer congestion if we attempt to impose upon it giant computers borrowed from disciplines and areas of activity remote from documentation. The present writer yields to no one in his belief that automation can, and will, make an important contribution to the reshaping of the librarian's profession and the improved utilization of the written word. But it must be an automation that is born of an understanding of what the library problem is, and what the librarian does, rather than a device, however precise its components, that superficially seems to imitate the behavior of the literature searcher. That books in a library can be inventoried according to certain characteristics of content and physical form, does not imply that the library problem is to be equated with the inventory problem. 'I have finished the plans for the new Columbia University Library,' said Stanford White, 'except that I haven't figured out where I'm going to put the damn books.' The information problem would be easy if it weren't for the damn books. The computer engineer can make an important contribution to the architecture of tomorrow's librarianship, but we cannot leave to him the solution of the problem of information retrieval, for he will not know what to do with the damn books. Always there are the damn books – everything must begin with them – they are the hard core of the library problem. In automation, as in architecture, form must follow function, and in its bibliographic applications it still has a considerable distance to go before it catches up. The closing of this 'gap' is the task of the new librarians.

7: *New Tools for Easing the Burden of Historical Research*

NO CONSCIENTIOUS historian, and let it not be suggested that there is any other, can stand before the severely classic façade of the National Archives without a feeling of frustration if not, indeed, of actual fright. The accelerated growth in the accumulation of the record of the human adventure probably can be measured by no man. The impressive achievement that is the *Monumenta Germaniae Historica* fades into relative insignificance in this day when the private papers of one public figure alone constitute an entire library. What a 'cinch' the Greek historians had!

'A few books', by which Lord Morley meant any number under five thousand, may, as Winston S. Churchill says, 'give a sense of comfort and even complacency', but a library or archive, filled with the vast and infinitely varied record the human race has succeeded in generating and preserving, gives to the historian no such feelings of security. Our colleagues, the scientists, pale before a growing Everest of technical literature. To be sure, *Chemical Abstracts* annually pours forth more than 85,000 synopses of chemical literature, and its current decennial index fills nineteen ponderous volumes, for the rate of publication in chemistry has increased ten-fold during the past half century. There are today some twenty thousand journals in biology, and thirty-five thousand in geography. But the scientist is really a very lucky fellow, for he needs only the literature *about* science. So too, the lawyer needs recourse only to the literature *of* and *about* legal matters, and the physician is concerned only with the writings *about* medicine. How simple life would be for the historian if he were interested only in writings *about* history, and his library

Presented before the Mississippi Valley Historical Association, Denver, Colorado, 1959. Originally published in *American Documentation*, Vol. 10 (October 1959), pp. 274–277.

were composed only of files of the historical reviews – how simple, and how dull! The historian cannot live by the bread of historiography alone. In contrast to the scientist, the historian must deal with all past human thought and action, and his library is that vast and diverse store of knowledge, experience, and wisdom that this and all preceding civilizations and cultures have accumulated and preserved.

To these monumental problems in bibliography, and to a growing specialization in historical inquiry, even the great promise of team research is but a partial solution. A corps of experts can fruitfully bring to bear upon an historical problem the collective power of their several specialities, but even they cannot rise above the effectiveness of the bibliographic apparatus by which they are supported and with which they must deal. And let us admit frankly that our bibliographic and library techniques are obsolete and inadequate to the burden of modern scholarship that we ask them to bear.

Knee-deep in paper and facing a rising tide, what, then, is the historian to do? It would seem obvious that he must look somewhere for succor. Today science is providing machines that will extend man's intellectual powers as, in a previous generation, they did his physical capabilities. This transition quite naturally raises problems of intellectual and psychological adjustment, and cries against 'the mechanization of scholarship' are everywhere heard in the land. But just as the laborer who would not make use of the lever or the pulley would properly be regarded as a very foolish person, so the historian who is unwilling to utilize to the full the tools which science can place before him would be a very stupid scholar.

There is nothing new in the historian's dependence upon the implements of science. In the 1930s, to choose one example, Robert C. Binkley was experimenting with a Leica camera and positive emulsion film as a means for recording the rare materials of scholarship in micro-photographic form – pioneering in a technique that today is universally taken for granted by the historian. At about the same time Edgar J. Goodspeed, the great Biblical scholar of the University of Chicago, wrote the *Curse in the Colophon*, an academic mystery tale, written (as he himself has told the present writer) partly for personal amusement, but even more to convince his associates in Classical studies of the importance of ultra-violet and infra-red light to the deciphering of palimpsests and other uses in the science of paleography. Extensive experimentation has also been carried out in the development of special optical devices for the comparison of conjugate texts; and all of us are more or less familiar with the use of Carbon 14 in establishing the antiquity of artifacts.

There would, then, seem to be no legitimate reason for the neglect by the librarian and the bibliographer of any new tools which science might place at his command, so long as it can be established that such instruments can increase the efficiency of his work and open doors of scholarship which have heretofore been closed. Now that the age of the computer seems to be firmly established, it would seem the better part of wisdom to take advantage of the capabilities of computer-like devices and skills of the computer engineer in the development of systems that increase the speed and accuracy of those repetitive tasks implicit in the storage and retrieval of bibliographic information. Thus the human brain can be reserved for those intellectual tasks which it and only it can perform.

The use of neo-mechanical devices for bibliographic manipulation is not unknown to the historian. At least some individual historians have been using edge-notched punched cards for the more flexible organization of their private files. The relatively simple coding that the limited fields of these cards permits often offers marked advantages over traditional subject headings. They can even be designed so as to free the user from the constant necessity for re-alphabetization and inter-filing. But these primitive techniques are, at best, limited in their effectiveness to relatively small collections, probably not in excess of ten thousand items, and even the simple mechanical devices for efficient manipulation do not increase their capacities to any appreciable extent. Still, an ingenious code and the skilful use of a knitting needle can accomplish surprising results if the demands are not too great.

An even less sophisticated system is the so-called Peek-a-Boo technique in which the passage of light through coincident holes in the card makes possible the co-ordination of related material. In this system the card represents the subject, not the bibliographic entry, and holes are punched in it to indicate those documents which are relevant. Thus, coincidence of holes, through which light can be sighted, identifies a reference which relates to the terms for which each, or all, of the cards stands. This system is, therefore, no more than a crude mechanical method for the traditional word index. The coincidence of *Dogs* and *Diseases* will identify an entry relating to the diseases of dogs, but it will not help much with such reversable compounds as Blind Venetian, and it is completely inarticulate when confronted with the Diet of Worms.

The seeming wizardry and obvious power of the big computers – the so-called 'giant brains', the Remington–Rand Univac, and the IBM series, to mention but a few, have long intrigued librarians. In some situations, particularly in industries where they are already available, they have through 'brute force' been adapted to bibliographic searching. But their capabilities for such purposes are more apparent than real: their programming is complicated and time-consuming; they are not designed for the logical operations that bibliographic work requires; their initial cost, or rental, is excessive; and they are encumbered with capabilities which, though quite appropriate to mathematical operations, are of no value whatever in information retrieval. One does not need a wheel to crush a butterfly.

The ideal mechanism for servicing the materials of research will come, not from the adaptation of existing machines to library problems, but through the development of devices designed specifically for bibliographic purposes. Somewhat more than ten years ago Ralph R. Shaw, then librarian of the U.S. Department of Agriculture, experimented with a device by means of which a microfilm bearing both document text and a code pattern of alternating opaque and transparent dots, was spun past a light source which activated a photo-electric cell, or failed to activate it, depending upon whether or not the patterns on the spinning film matched the pattern, symbolizing the subject being sought, that was interposed between the light sources and the photo-electric cell. But the capabilities of the Shaw Rapid Selector were severely limited, and it was never mechanically perfected. In Paris, about the same time, Cordonnier developed a similar technique, and Jacques Samain is now marketing his Filmo-Rex. At the present time, however, the ultimate in the microfilm technique is the Minicard system developed by Eastman Kodak for the U.S. Air Force. This is an almost unbelievably precise combination of mechanical, electronic, and optical components which manipulate, for purposes of literature searching, bits of microfilm approximately the size of a special delivery stamp, which contain both text and code pattern. The great advantage of this system is that the entire text, in microfilm (approximately 60 × reduction), can be transported through the entire searching operation and enlarged to normal size at the end. This obviates the necessity of referring to a document file or a library stack when the answer to the search has been achieved. Eastman will accept orders from any department of history at a price probably somewhere between one and two million dollars exclusive of the educational discount. Nevertheless, one must admit that the Minicard does represent an important technological advance in mechanizing the storage and retrieval of bibliographic data.

H. P. Luhn of the International Business Machines Corporation has also done developmental work in this field, using, of course, punched cards. The Luhn Scanner represented one of his earlier devices, which was followed by the IBM X794 which never went farther than the drawing boards. Finally, there is the system developed at Western Reserve University, designed specifically for literature searching.

The limitations of a discussion such as this preclude the possibility of any extensive description of the devices mentioned above, but perhaps enough has been said to indicate the rapidity with which this new field is developing. One should emphasize that scarcely more than fifteen years have elapsed since the present writer, then with the Office of Strategic Services, began to experiment with IBM equipment in primitive attempts to index intelligence reports. Most of the development has taken place since 1950, and there is every indication that this activity will accelerate rapidly in the years immediately ahead. In librarianship and bibliographic methods generally, a real revolution is in the making – a revolution that was anticipated in 1937, with unusual foresight, by Frederick J. Keppel of the Carnegie Corporation when he wrote:

As to cataloging cards . . . I blush to think how many years we watched the so-called business machines juggle with pay-rolls and bank books before it occurred to us that they might be adapted to dealing with library cards with equal dexterity.

Indexing has become an entirely new art. The modern index is no longer bound up in the volume, but remains on cards, and the modern version of the old Hollerith machine will sort out and photograph anything that the dial tells it. . . .We librarians must keep up with all these applications of science.

But because there is widespread misunderstanding of the nature of these new tools for easing the bibliographic burden of the research worker, it is important to review, even briefly, the functions of these machines, what may be expected from them, and their limitations, as well as their meaning for the historian.

Obviously, their primary function is to perform the tedious repetitive operations of literature searching and document analysis more rapidly, more accurately, and at a lower cost than is now possible with traditional library methods. They must be able to relate, compare, and otherwise correlate the information fed to them in ways comparable to those functions of the human brain. Their memories must not be subject to the human error of forgetfulness. They must be able to deal with both specific and generic terms and to relate the one to the other. They must operate on several semantic levels, for though much of the meaning of documents is conveyed by isolates alone, relations are also important in revealing the subject content of documents. They must be mechanically dependable, and they must be available at a cost that is not astronomical but within reach of at least the larger research centers. One may assume, and with reason, that in the not-far-distant future they will be within the budget of the average college library.

But to turn to the other side of the coin, what is it that these machines are not? Certainly they are *not* substitutes for the human brain, and they will *not* free any scholar from the burden of concentrated thinking. They will search, but they will not perform *re*search. They will answer the scholar's questions only when those questions are properly framed and expressed. They will not put the librarian or the bibliographer out of business but on the contrary, they can raise his profession to new levels of intellectual achievement. But by the same token, the librarians and bibliographers of the future must prepare themselves to meet the new challenge of these machines – automotive engineering did not grow out of the livery stable.

These new machines are tools, not robots. Thirty years ago Karl Young was wont to tell his students at Yale that 'scholarship depends as much on one's legs as it does on one's head', by which he meant that in research a deal of drudgery must precede the fullest utilization of the scholar's intellectual powers. In a very real sense these machines are the 'legs' of the scholar, and by easing the physical burden of the historian, they can free his mind for those creative processes it, and only it, can perform.

One need not remind an audience of historians that innovation and invention must always push hard against the inertia of society. This is as it should be, for only thus can the permanent and the effective be winnowed from the chaff of the trivial and inconsequential. But if an innovation is a thing of substance and virtue, society eventually does yield. In many quarters scholars and librarians alike distrust, and even fear, these new machines with an intensity that is born of misunderstanding and insecurity. Doubtless the librarian–scholars of the Alexandriana were dismayed when the use of parchment as a writing surface broke the embargo on papyrus and thus destroyed for ever the Egyptian monopoly on books. Doubtless, too, the imaginative soul who first ruthlessly cut his parchment scroll into fragments and tied them together at the back to form a codex was viewed by his contemporaries as an idiotic vandal. Some evidence survives to suggest that the scribes looked askance at Gutenberg and his contemporaries, who were liberally stamping out books in multiple copies with a speed unbelievable to those accustomed to manual transcription. Probably all of us here can remember the struggle to establish the social respectability of photo-offset printing from typewritten composition. Even yet there are those who stubbornly insist that a book that isn't manufactured in the tradition sanctified by Gutenberg and Mergenthaler really isn't 'printed'. Admittedly, the machines that have here been so hastily reviewed are still in the Gutenbergian stage, but they are a reality and even in their present imperfect form their practicability has been proved. Doubtless every historian has sighed for the day when he could procure the data he needs with a metaphorical clap of the hands. This day is not yet here, but its advent is, perhaps, no more incredible than would have been the typewriter to those who wrote in cunieform on tablets of clay.

8: *Librarians' Pugwash, or* Intrex *on the Cape*

INTREX, for the enlightenment of the uninitiated, is an acronym for *information transfer experiments* and, parenthetically, one might note that in the most *avant-garde* engineering circles information is no longer communicated or even retrieved, it is transferred. But whatever one may think of the semantic derivation of INTREX, the term stands for a projected multi-million-dollar four-year research program at the Massachusetts Institute of Technology, to be directed toward the development of new methods for technical and scientific information handling. Librarians of the twenty-first century will then be enabled to deal effectively with the mounting flood of paper that threatens to inundate the world of research. Intrepid INTREXians characterize this documentation crisis as a 'knowledge explosion', and thus assume a positive correlation between the proliferation of print and the increment of man's understanding of the world in which he lives.

The INTREX idea seems to have been strongly influenced by the early prognostications of Vannevar Bush and the more recent explorations of J. C. R. Licklider[1] into applications (expected by the year 2000) of the technology of advanced data processing to library systems design. Thus INTREX is seen by its advocates as 'an on-line computer-based complex of devices . . . a sort of rapid-access knowledge network . . . easily available to users'[2] and

[1] J. C. R. Licklider. *Libraries of the future.* MIT Press, Cambridge, Mass., 1965
[2] MIT press release, April 25, 1965. An 'on-line' computer is one that is connected by cable, often a telephone cable, to one or more consoles located at remote points. A console is a typewriter, or Flexowriter, modified to serve as a device for transmitting instructions to the computer and printing out its responses.

perhaps not unlike the experimental MAC-TIP Project developed by M. M. Kessler and others of the MIT staff.[3] Although the project is centered in the School of Engineering, by utilizing as fully as possible the entire MIT community as an experimental and technical resource for developing INTREX, its architects expect 'that the resulting new library complex will be in operation by the 1970's'.[4]

To support a planning conference for the purpose of formulating for MIT a coordinated program of research and experimentation that would result in 'a design for evolving a large university library into an information transfer system', The Independence Foundation of Philadelphia generously provided the sum of almost $200,000. This five-week conference, which met from August 2 to September 3, 1965, at the Summer Studies' Center of the National Academy of Science at Woods Hole, Mass., was strictly limited to invited participants selected for their competence in such appropriate fields as engineering, computer technology, linguistics, publishing, librarianship, and library education, Carl F. J. Overhage, professor of engineering at MIT and director of Project INTREX, served as chairman of the conference, which was divided into three parts. During the first two weeks a small planning group (composed of the MIT INTREX staff with the addition of Herman H. Fussler of the University of Chicago, Herman H. Henkle of the John Crerar Library, Chicago, Ill., J. C. R. Licklider of IBM, Stephen A. McCarthy of Cornell University, and Foster E. Mohrhardt of the National Library of Agriculture)* which was joined from time to time by other specialists, prepared the preliminary working papers for consideration and debate by the total assembly of participants, who converged upon Woods Hole for the third week of August. During the following two weeks the planning group prepared the final report, which will be published by the MIT Press.[5] The present writer's

[3] M. M. Kessler. 'The MIT Technical Information Project', *Physics Today*, Vol. 18, March 1965, pp. 28-36.

[4] R. M. Fano. *The MAC System: A Progress Report*. Massachusetts Institute of Technology, Cambridge, Mass., 1964. MAC-TR 12.

[5] *Editor's Note:* Subsequent to the writing of Dr. Shera's paper, this report

---

* The writer must apologize for any inacuracies in the listing of the planning group. The personnel of this group was never formally made public, and we must depend entirely upon observation and memory.

participation in the deliberations was limited to the third week, when some 30 invited specialists, designated as 'visitors', made such contributions as they were able to the criticism and amplification of the formulations that had been prepared by their predecessors.

This third week opened with a general review of the progress that had been made up to that point in identifiying areas of needed research. Most of the week was devoted to a series of concurrent committee meetings, each under the direction of a member of the planning group, devoted to such problems as: advanced systems concepts, annotated catalogs; access; image storage; browsing; and the economic aspects of the information transfer problem. Though the visitors were assigned to particular committees, they were free (and even encouraged) to divide their time among the groups according to their interests or competences. Also, each visitor was assigned at least one problem on which he was supposed to prepare a written statement; the present writer's question, for example, dealt with methods for evaluating information transfer systems.

Each visitor was provided with a very substantial volume of mimeographed documents generated either by the INTREX project staff or by the planning group, and during the week the several working committees generated much more. The urge to 'rush into print' seemed to be endemic in the visitors. Never have so many written so much for so few (a curiously paradoxical phenomenon in a conference presumably devoted to discovering means for controling the rising tide of paper)! But perhaps the participants were deliberately trying to precipitate a paper crisis to dramatize its dangers,

Throughout the conference the MAC-TIP system was on exhibition, but like most such devices when their sponsors are most eager for effective performance, it was completely recalcitrant and uncooperative, so we were never able to 'carry on a dialogue' with it. Nevertheless, enough evidence was available to suggest that the system could, within its limitations, become quite a powerful bibliographic tool.

The week ended with a plenary session, addressed informally by

has been made available: Carl F. J. Overhage and R. Joyce Harmon, eds. *INTREX: The Report of a Planning Conference on Information Transfer Experiments, September 3, 1965.* MIT Press, Cambridge, Mass., 1965, xviii—276 pp., $5.

Vannevar Bush, at which the 'findings' of the several committees were presented. On September 7, four days after the planning group had completed its task, MIT released a summary of the conference recommendations.

The conference devoted particular attention to 'three major streams of progress in the information transfer field' as being especially significant in shaping the research libraries and information centres of the future: '(*a*) the modernization of current library procedures through the application of technical advances in data processing, textual storage, and reproduction; (*b*) the growth, largely under federal sponsorship, of a national network of libraries and other information centres; and (*c*) the extension of the rapidly developing technology of on-line interacting computer communities into the domains of the library and other information centres.',[6] The belief was expressed that the potentially great advantages to libraries of the rapidly emerging advances in computer technology can be realized only if the technology is supported by the materials resources of the modern research library and by the integration of local and national bibliographic and information networks.

Though discussions extended over a wide range of possible experiments that might reasonably absorb the attention of the INTREX staff, the recommended program that eventually emerged was, in the main, concentrated upon the problem of *access*: particularly access to bibliographic materials, documents, and data banks. A 'core research program' dealing with the problem of access, together with supporting activities and extensions, was formulated.

A Model Experimental Library

The first recommended step was the establishment of a model experimental library to provide a realistic environment for pilot operations. In this model library could be observed and examined most of the basic procedures common to university and research libraries, and conventional methods could be used as controls for the new computor technology. The materials in the model library would be sufficient, in both number and variety, to provide valid experimental data without sacrificing ready manipulability.

[6] 'Project INTREX Planning Conference. Summary of Report', September 2, 1965., p.1.

The conference conceived the catalog as being central to the information system and therefore recommended the development of a computerized 'augmented catalog' that should 'encompass an inter-disciplinary field that should contain references to enough materials to interest a serious worker and to present significant bibliographic problems'. The catalog should be compatible with an on-line computer system and, in addition to making possible searches for both known and unknown documents, should provide experimental data for the investigation of problems in selection, acquisition, selective dissemination, browsing, the recording of use, and related library problems.

The need to determine the merits of the various approaches to the reproduction and display of text in terms of their respective effectiveness and cost was pointed out by the conferees. Valid tests are needed for evaluating the available methods of photographic reproduction, television display, and other means for providing the user with access to the materials retrieved by the bibliographic system. Problems of storage, as well as display, should be investigated, since they also relate to access.

Project INTREX was urged to explore a wide range of ideas for the promotion of an integrated network of university and and research libraries that would be national, and eventually international, in scope. Also emphasized was the need for cooperation with existing agencies such as the National Library of Medicine, the National Aeronautics and Space Administration, and bibliographic, abstracting, and documentation organizations, with a particular view to avoiding competition and duplication and to promoting standards of procedure and format. The conference expressed concern over the tendency of experiments in information retrieval to focus upon the document as the main information unit, and therefore proposed research into the practicability of 'computerized data handbooks' and data banks.

Other areas for possible future investigation were identified as: (*a*) 'teaching and learning' in on-line networks; (*b*) browsing and planned facilities to foster unplanned discovery; (*c*) selective dissemination of information; (*d*) use of the on-line network to expedite preparing, reviewing, printing, indexing, and abstracting of manuscripts, and (*e*) 'publishing' through the system to the on-line community. The conference expressed concern over 'the primitive state of two critical items: consoles and interacting languages', since both are basic to the success of an on-line computer-oriented network. Finally, the conference pointed to the need for a 'unifying theory that will lead to coherent design and interpretation of experiments in information transfer systems' as providing a challenge to the INTREX staff.

The program set forth by the conference, even when it is generalized and superficially summarized as of necessity it has been in this review, is impressive. Proof of success must, of course, await execution. There was some grumbling among the visitors that they were being asked to do MIT thinking for them, but most of us found the meetings at Woods Hole an exhilarating and exciting intellectual experience in which we probably received more than we gave. Not the least of its accomplishments was that it brought together several diverse groups which are not normally in contact with each other, and despite the fact that at the outset there were some rather serious problems in communication, the engineers learned that there is much more to library problems than simple data processing, while the librarians perceived a new world of computer technology with almost unlimited potentialities.

Weaknesses of the Conference

But the conference was not without its weaknesses; no conference is. It is unfortunate that Project INTREX is so deeply committed to the on-line computer, for we are not ready to accept the belief that MAC-TIP necessarily exemplifies the shape of things to come. Moreover, we regret the absence of the reference librarians, whose collective years of experience could have added much to the correction of assumptions and misconceptions about the nature of the information transfer process. If librarianship is more than the fetching and carrying of books, so the work of the reference librarian, the true information retriever, is much more than the simple action of producing data on demand. So obsessed were some of the conferees with the beauties of a bright new online computerized world that one engineer saw in the emergence of 'computerized text' the demise of publishing like 'the whaling industry of Nantucket'; and the committee on browsing, after a lengthy and rather silly debate, envisaged a system of long-distance library browsing by television! Perhaps in the excitement and stimulation of the occasion we all become a little punch-drunk from the impact of the new technology and the vision of a world in which the engineer-librarian would be king.

We regret, too, the failure of the meeting to take into account the intellectual, psychological, and behavioral patterns of the library user. We noted the absence of any specialists in brain physiology and neural research, and only passing mention was made of the need to train users in the techniques and skills of library use. Quite properly, we thought, Victor Yngve warned of the dangers and pitfalls in natural language used in conjunction with the computor, but his observation passed almost unnoticed. To have acknowledged his point would have shaken the commitment of INTREX to its very foundations. In many ways the assumptions of the participants were as naive and lacking in demonstrable fact as those of the pioneers in conventional librarianship.

Yet one inescapable conclusion emerges. Despite the fact that the topography of the future is obscured by yet undispelled fog, as the contours of Martha's Vineyard are shrouded by the mists of early morning, unquestionably there are tides running, and currents moving beneath the surface, that can dramatically reshape the coastline of librarianship so familiar to us today. The librarian can blind himself to these changes in his environment and follow the sabre-toothed tiger into extinction; or he can see in them the vision of a new heaven and a new earth with boundless opportunities for extended and more effective service, and with them, almost unlimited enrichment of the intellectual content of his professional practice.

9: *Effect of Machine Methods on the Organization of Knowledge*

IN THE wake of any social or technological innovation there comes, almost inevitably, a backwash of action and reaction in which the invention is esteemed as a perfect panacea that will cure even more ills than it was designed to alleviate, or in which it is condemned as an instrument of evil destined only to intensify those very problems it was meant to solve. Subsequent experience usually demonstrates that the truth lies somewhere between these extremes, but this repetitive pattern of emotional reaction still persists. To such responses innovations in library procedures and operations are scarcely immune. The historian of American librarianship can testify to their attendance upon the introduction of the card catalog, the subject classification of books, and especially upon the introduction of such mechanisms as the microfilm and the microcard.

Today we seem to be on the brink of startling new developments in the field of high-speed manipulation of large masses of bibliographic data, and already the emotional responses are becoming apparent. On the one hand, there are those who foresee a complete 'industrial revolution' in librarianship that will raise the profession to new heights of accomplishment and make possible the realization of bibliographic efficiency undreamed of by any previous generation. On the other hand, there are those, especially the catalogers, who recoil in terror lest someone discover that machines are 'smarter' than they, and who fear technological obsolescence. Both reactions, of course, are implicit and excessive tributes to the effectiveness of this new technology.

One can argue that we do not as yet know enough about the precise nature of the new mechanisms, and that our perspective

Originally published in *American Documentation*, Vol. 3 (January 1952), pp. 15-20.

is as yet inadequate for a dispassionate appraisal of the effect of machine methods on the organization of knowledge. However, it is not excessive to maintain that we can even now envisage the general characteristics of these mechanisms with sufficient clarity to enable us to hypothesize certain conservative estimates of their effects upon traditional bibliographic procedures and operations, especially as these relate to bibliographic classification.

What, then, are the characteristics of these mechanisms? (1) They will probably be electronic rather than mechanical. (2) They will doubtless make use of photographic techniques in one or more forms. (3) They will be capable of storing large masses of bibliographic data in their 'memories'. (4) Through the operation of a coding system they will be able to sort this stored data in a variety of ways so that the user receives only those materials relevant to his purpose. (5) They can be designed to manipulate complete bibliographic units (i.e., complete photographic copies of entire monographs or other documents); abstracts of these units; bibliographic information only; or fragmented segments of information (i.e., units of information or units of thought). (6) They will operate at speeds far in excess of the human. (7) Negatively, they will not be mechanical substitutes for human intelligence. Hence, (8) their use seems likely to be limited to the more complex problems of bibliographic searching, and therefore, they may not be applicable to the entire range of bibliothecal operations.

This brief capitulation emphasizes the enormous potential inherent in these machines, and the difficulties encountered when one attempts to discuss them with restraint. Even a conservative view must acknowledge that here are latent forces that could revolutionize, not only traditional library and bibliographic operations but the very pattern of scholarship itself. Therefore, any understanding of the significance of these machines for our present methods of organizing recorded knowledge must begin with an examination of the changes which they may bring to the methods by which the scholar of the future will operate.

Initial enthusiasm for these machines as instruments of bibliographic manipulation must not obscure the fundamental fact that they were originally designed to expedite the operations of research, and that it is in this field, rather than in librarianship or documentation, that the most startling future developments are likely to be found. Through the use of these machines the scholar ought, not only to save himself countless hours of drudgery, but actually to extend his powers to manipulate accurately the raw data of research in ways beyond the limitations of the human brain.

Therefore, it was in the physical sciences and certain of the biological sciences associated with them, that the great values of machines became most conspicuously apparent. This is true not only because the materials of research in the sciences are the most nearly exact and precise but also because in their extensive reliance upon mathematical symbols they had a language peculiarly adapted to the inherent nature of the new machines. One need not elaborate here the importance of machines to the scholarship of science; indeed, one can hardly pick up a scientific journal without finding a discussion of the application of electronic techniques in some new way to the investigation of physical or biological phenomena.

Less apparent but no less real, is the importance of these techniques for the social sciences. A relatively long period of limited use of mechanical calculating and sorting devices, from the simple adding machine to the most elaborate variants of the Hollerith principle, are clues to what the future may hold. The electronic mechanisms are not only capable of performing complicated mathematical operations with great speed and precision but they also make possible the 'collective description' of social phenomena, the accumulation of masses of social statistics, and other 'raw data' pertinent to the study of society. To state the possibilities somewhat more dramatically, these machines can eventually serve the social scientist as a laboratory, an archive of the materials of research, a depository of the *materia sociologica* for his particular investigation, and a library for the organization of his professional literature.

The utility of assemblages of social data to the scholar is familiar enough, but recent developments in statistical theory indicate that such assemblages will also be a conspicuously important part of the materials required for the promotion of commerce and industry. Traditionally, the central problem of statistics has been to make possible statistical inferences, to derive reasonably secure statements on the basis of incomplete, but reliably sampled, information. Through the work of the late Abraham Wald and others, however, it now seems possible that statistical probability may be validly applied to the decision-making processes of business and government. This new theory of statistical decision,[1] if and when it becomes firmly established among the procedures of commercial and industrial enterprise, will extend the utility of these collections of raw social data beyond the study of the academician to the executive and administrative offices of manufacturing and trade. The social utility of the new mechanisms, then, is not only a matter of scholarship, as it is generally understood, but an important new development that will bring the work of the librarian–documentalist closer to the market-place than he has ever been before.

But before any of these innovations can be fully realized the social scientist must follow the lead of his natural science colleague in developing both a standardized terminology, that will be acceptable to, and adopted by, a consensus of the entire profession, and a symbolic language capable of translating the relationships of social phenomena into precise formulations appropriate to the requirements of the machines themselves.

From this brief description it can be readily seen that in the world of scholarship the new mechanisms, when developed to their fullest capabilities, would form a bond among the producers, the consumers, and the librarian–documentalists. Traditionally, library operations and schemes for the organization of the literature of scholarship have been predicated on the implicit assumption that the book, or some variant or derivative of the code form, is the standard bibliographic unit. From the foregoing, however, it is apparent that this is no longer necessarily so. Not the least significant contribution that these machines can make to the organization of recorded knowledge is their promise of freedom from the tyranny of the codex to the degree that Dana's dream of a 'library without books', could be a reality.

All this is not mere idle speculation nor is it wishful thinking about the possibilities of a labor-saving device that will be at the disposal of the librarian's convenience. It reaches down to, and forces a complete reorientation of, the very philosophy of librarianship itself. Released from the need to organize physical objects, 'books', the librarian will not only discover that his system

---

[1] L. J. Savage, 'The Theory of Statistical Decision', *Journal of the American Statistical Association*, Vol. 46 (March 1951), pp. 55–67.

for the organization of library materials will now approach more closely to the organization of pure knowledge, but he will be at liberty to reorganize his basic schematism or employ as many variant or supplementary schematisms, as his operations and needs dictate. Thus the classification of knowledge will not be a fixed and unalterable pattern, based on *a priori* assumptions regarding the most nearly logical arrangement of books on the shelves, but a series of quite widely varying schematisms, each constructed for a specific purpose, or purposes, in accordance with a particular point of view or philosophic orientation.

In the light of the foregoing generalizations and observations, it may be well to examine, in somewhat more detail, four major aspects or segments of the field of bibliographic organization, viz.: (1) patterns of bibliography, both enumerative and subject; (2) bibliothecal operations, with reference to institutional structure and internal organization; (3) personnel; and (4) professional training.

Up to the present the problems of developing complete national bibliography (enumerative bibliography) have been largely regarded as distinct from those of subject bibliography, and the interdependence of each, though it was recognized, was held to be relatively slight. Failure to recognize this basic relationship has been a costly blunder, but it was a *natural* error which derived from the chaos of our present bibliographic system, and the lack of an effectively co-ordinated and well-planned attack upon bibliographic problems. Through the medium of these new mechanisms, national enumerative bibliography and subject bibliography are brought more closely together than they have ever been before, and the relationship between them will become apparent as well as real. Through the application of machine techniques true national bibliography not only becomes economically feasible, but it emerges as an essential foundation of adequate subject analysis. Through the techniques of electronic 'storage' national bibliography becomes available for manipulation in an almost infinite variety of subject analyses. Such freedom of subject access is wellnigh impossible in a world in which the bibliographer is chained to the codex (the book or its physical representation in catalog card or bibliography entry) as the bibliographic unit.

The implications of these machine methods for bibliothecal

operations are even more striking. For the moment it appears that the costs and complexity of these machines preclude their use in any but the most elaborate and intricate bibliographic operations. This necessitates a very high degree of centralization of bibliographic operation and reference work. This in turn presupposes the creation of one, or at most no more than a very few, national bibliographic centers with extensive resources and facilities for the assimilation, analysis, and dissemination of bibliographic information. Such centers would then become great foci of bibliographic activity, as rich in resources as it is humanly possible to make them. But suppose the costs of electronic manipulation are materially reduced so that even the smaller institutions have access to these machines, what then? Obviously, the answer is that, though the national centers for bibliographic assimilation and analysis will likely still persist, at least the reference and research functions can be decentralized and the local units can service the results of these bibliographic operations in ways that best meet their local needs. Here, one can envisage something like a national central library, or libraries, with a system of outlying libraries which maintain close contact with the bibliographic requirements of scholarship. Such an institutional structure could be informal as well as formal, but in either case the relationship between the foci and peripherac would be one of mutual interdependence.

Within the limitations of the present discussion it is obviously impossible to consider all the implications of machine methods for the internal structure and organization of the library, but perhaps some awareness of the impact of these innovations can be gained from a consideration of their effect upon library classification. Again, two possible extremes may be hypothesized. One may assume, for example, that the importance of the machines may surpass even the most optimistic expectations of their inventors, to the point that they completely supersede the codex as the graphic record of human experience, and that books and their derivatives may become, at least so far as bibliothecal problems are concerned, as obsolete as the papyrus roll or the clay tablet. Bibliothecal classification, as it is known today, would completely disappear. Under such circumstances the classification problem would then center about the 'unit of knowledge', rather than about the problem of arranging physical objects (books). Rolls of film, or whatever other medium was employed to 'feed' the machines, would survive as the only physical entities requiring subject arrangement, and for such purposes very broad and general groupings would suffice. Admittedly this is an extreme view, but it does emphasize the effect of these mechanisms upon the need for the analysis of literature in terms of the meaningful 'thought unit' and the identification of such units in utilitarian and pragmatic terms. Classification, then, could depart from the traditional form of the Comtean hierarchy of the sciences, and focus attention upon the devising of a variety of codes, appropriate to the capacities of the machine, which would yield to the user the desired information in each broad field.

At the other extreme one may hypothesize a situation in which these mechanisms are supplements to, rather than substitutes for, the codex. Here, the problem of library classification would likely retain at least part of its more familiar pattern, and the extent of divergence would depend upon the degree to which machine methods were employed for the analysis of book content. But even the conservative view seems to foreshadow the decline of bibliothecal classification as it is now familiar to the librarian, for even the more crude machines seem to promise more efficient subject access to book content than is possible with the most nearly perfect book classification. Thus freed of the responsibility for subject analysis, book classification could be limited to either arrangement in broad subject groupings, or even a simple mnemonic schematism, having little more than locational value.

But whatever the impact of these new devices upon bibliothecal practice, one thing seems certain, they will make mandatory an analysis of the graphic record into its component thought-units of varying degrees of magnitude and depth, and the organization of these units into meaningful categories that will vary from time to time and place to place according to the needs and abilities of major user-groups.

Though there is nothing esoteric about the concept 'thought unit', it has been subject to such widespread misunderstanding that a brief explanation may here be appropriate. The thought unit, as it is here used, is nothing more than the verbal expression of an idea or a fact, which in turn is a constellation of constituent ideas or facts, and the magnitude of the thought unit varies directly with the depth of analysis employed in its isolation or identification.

F. H. Giddings, in his treatment of the scientific scrutiny of social facts, has admirably clarified this phenomenon with respect to social data and the uses that the social scientist makes of them.

'The particular instance of something or other which has arrested our attention looks like a unit or item, detached or detachable, and so we think of it for the moment. Then we make further discoveries. Our instance is a unit as far as its relations with other instances like itself or different happen to go, but if we leave them out of our field of vision and forget them, and look intently at our particular instance we see it resolve into a number of lesser items, arranged perhaps in clusters or patterns, and like enough, moving about. Each of these items in turn, we presently ascertain, is composite, and so on, without end.' Giddings continues with an illustration. 'The social scientist', he says, 'may be interested chiefly in a mill town, or chiefly in a neighborhood, or chiefly in certain families. At one time he will be most concerned about what the mill town or the neighborhood or a family *does*. At another time he will be more concerned about what it *is*. As long as he is attending to what the mill town does he thinks of it as a whole. It is a community. He compares it with other communities as wholes. He observes similarities and differences of activity and achievement. These observations may lead him to ask why such similarities and differences exist, how they are to be accounted for. Trying to answer this question, he finds himself inquiring what his mill town is, and from that moment he is resolving it into components. He is discovering that it is made up of corporations, trade unions, churches, schools, shops and markets, professional men and business men, skilled mechanics and unskilled laborers, native born folk and foreign born folk of various nationalities; in fine, of inhabitants arranged in bewildering clusters and patterns. If he is interested chiefly in a neighborhood or in a family he has a like experience. He thinks of it as a unit while he is learning what it does. He necessarily thinks of it as a composite when he tries to learn what it is.

'A particular instance, then, is a unit or not as we happen, or have occasion, to see it, and we have occasion to see it in the one or the other way according to the nature of the investigation that we attempt to make.'[2]

[2] F. H. Giddings, *The Scientific Study of Human Society* (Chapel Hill: University of North Carolina Press, 1924), pp. 44–45.

Similarly, G. J. Renier has said with reference to the methods of the historian: 'The human past consists of things that happened. There is no hierarchy among these occurrences . . . an occurrence remains an elusive phenomenon. It is never single, as I have pointed out, and . . . the apprehension of the occurrence by the human mind is in itself a mystery. . . . The historian, who is a pragmatist even if he does not know it, asks no more than to be allowed to behave as though his mind can get hold of occurrences which, by means of the linguistic symbols that stand for them, can be put into his story.'[3]

The librarian–documentalist, too, is a pragmatist, and in a sense a historian and social scientist, and though he cannot always reduce these molecular units of thought to their constituent atoms, at least he must be able to isolate them with sufficient precision to make them meaningful to his clientele, useful for the particular purpose in hand, and practicable within the managerial economics of his methods of operation. Though the scholar may need to vary these information or thought units according to his special needs, for the purpose of the indexer or classifier these units should re-occur with sufficient frequency to justify coding them as key concepts of the discipline.

This identification and classification of the vast array of concepts that constitute what is generally called knowledge is in itself a major research task involving several disciplines, among them logic, epistemology, and semantics, and though the resources of many other subject disciplines working co-operatively will be required to effect such a research program, it is the major task of the librarian to see that the job gets done. This will be a new and dynamic rôle for the librarian but it is a responsibility that he dare not leave to others if he is to retain control of his profession.

Personnel and the training of personnel are so closely interrelated that they may best be considered simultaneously, and it is not enough merely to say that henceforth the librarian–documentalist must be skilled in the techniques of machine operation. We have already seen that machines alone, of and by themselves, will not solve our problems; imagination and intelligence are essential to their fullest utilization. This means that the future

[3] G. J. Renier, *History, Its Purpose and Method* (Boston: The Beacon Press, 1950), p. 94.

librarian must be a specialist in the discipline of bibliographic organization. Over and above a sound general education he must be thoroughly informed regarding the basic principles and techniques of librarianship; he must know the literature of some specific subject field or group of related subject fields; and above all he must comprehend the uses to which the literature of these fields is put. He need not be a practitioner of research himself, though a certain proportion of his colleagues should be so trained, but he must be familiar with, and able to interpret the research that has been done; and he must understand the limitations which existing knowledge imposes upon him and the changes in production and use of graphic records which accompany advances in the methods of scholarship. Finally, it is the responsibility of the library schools to provide such training.

This suggestion is not as radical as one might, at first, suppose. Already there is scattered evidence that those charged with the training of librarians are beginning, however modestly, to think in these terms, and to paraphrase Thomas Carlyle, 'Gad, they'd better!' The documentalists are in full cry for a training system of their own, that will meet their 'peculiar' needs. But the librarians need the precision of the documentalists, and the documentalists, on their part, need the breadth of viewpoint of the librarian. Both can gain much from consolidation, and neither can 'go it alone'.

In a 1952 issue of the *Saturday Review of Literature*, a group of selected librarians of large municipal public libraries report on the reference questions put to them by their constituents during the past year.[4] But in these summaries there is precious little to inspire the respect or support of the body politic, and much to arouse the contempt of the scholar – an all too eloquent testimony to the intellectual bankruptcy that threatens the library profession. From just such a morass of petty 'services' these new mechanisms promise a real escape.

Librarianship need offer no sniveling apology for its existence. In the manifold problems that constitute the discipline of bibliographic organization the profession can find its own hard core of substance. These new machines do not prognosticate technological obsolescence for the librarian, if he will but take the trouble to direct them to the solution of his central problem – the organiza-

[4] Louis Shores, comp., 'What Americans Wanted to Know in 1951', *Saturday Review of Literature* (February 9, 1952), pp. 36–39.

tion and maximum utilization of our graphic records. Rather they are a kind of bibliothecal geiger counter that can reveal the latent forces that lie below the surface. Or, to change the metaphor, a *deus ex machina* that can save librarians from their own seemingly determined self-destruction.

Admittedly much of what has been said here is speculative, certainly a great deal of it depends upon detailed developments the exact nature of which we can now but dimly foresee. But the general pattern seems clear, and perhaps it will not prove to have been mere idle speculation if from this attenuated panorama we achieve a measure of insight into, and understanding of, our future tasks.

10: *Common Languages in Librarianship and Documentation*

1. LANGUAGE AND KNOWLEDGE

'The most momentous and at the same time the most mysterious product of the human mind,' is Susanne K. Langer's tribute to the invention of language,[1] and certainly man's power to communicate with his fellows, either directly through the spoken word or indirectly by means of the graphic record, is his greatest achievement as a social being. Without it there could be no culture and upon it all the cognitive processes of the human intellect may be said to depend.[2] It is one segment of that part of the human condition which Hannah Arendt has called the Vita Activa, the web of relationships that is the human condition of plurality, the fact that men, not Man, live on the earth and inhabit the world.[3] A life without speech and without action is literally dead and has ceased to be a human life because it is no longer lived among men; for by word and deed man inserts himself into the human world, the world of men; these are the modes by which men reveal themselves to other men, not as physical objects but as individuals with unique personal identities. Thus the Romans used the words 'to be among men' (*inter homines esse*) and 'to cease to be among men' (*inter homines esse desinere*) as synonymous, respectively, with the verbs 'to live' and 'to die'.

It is this characteristic of language as the fabric of culture that has made it so difficult to comprehend. For language is more

[1] Susanne K. Langer, *Philosophy in a New Key* (Cambridge: Harvard University Press, 1942), p. 83.

[2] Jerome S. Bruner, Jacqueline J. Goodnow and George A. Austin, *A Study of Thinking* (New York: Wiley, 1956), pp. 10–11.

[3] Hannah Arendt, *The Human Condition* (Chicago: University of Chicago Press), pp. 7, 175–181.

Originally published in Allen Kent (ed.), *Information Retrieval and Machine Translation*, Vol. 2 (New York: Interscience Publishers, 1961), pp. 1051–1060.

than a simple vehicle for the communication of information, and, indeed, Miss Arendt argues that 'from the viewpoint of sheer utility', it would seem to be 'an awkward substitute for signs' as in mathematics words can be a poor substitute for symbols.[4] So, too, Miss Langer rejects the utilitarian notion that the essence of language is the communication of natural wants,[5] while accepting the belief that the motive of language is the transformation of experience into concepts and as being 'through and through symbolic, and only sometimes signific'.[6] This position, of course, does not deny the communicative function of language but it emphasizes rather, as Sapir has pointed out, that language is 'primarily a vocal actualization of the tendency to see reality symbolically'.[7] It is this symbolic quality that renders language a particularly effective instrument for communication which, in the actual give and take of social intercourse, has been refined and become complicated into the linguistic patterns that are familiar to us today. Thus Herskovitz has defined language as a system of arbitrary signs and vocal symbols by means of which members of a social group, or culture, are able to co-operate or interact.[8] Or, in the more esoteric definition of Charles Morris, language is 'a set of plurasituational signs with interpersonal significata common to members of an interpreter family, the signs being producible by means of the interpreter family, and combinable in some ways but not in others to form compound signs'.[9]

These referential language systems do not need speech for the preservation of their communicative power. The history of writing is a series of attempts, spreading over uncounted centuries, to develop an independent symbolism based on graphic representation. Effective systems of writing, then, whether alphabetic or not, are more or less exact transfers of speech, but the original language may maintain itself even in more or less remote transfers to quite different media; for example, the Morse telegraphic code. This coding may eventually, under conditions of sufficient refinement and sophistication, manifest itself as true symbolic patterns that can even substitute, within limitations, for speech

[4] Ibid., p. 179.   [5] Langer, op. cit., pp. 96–97.   [6] Ibid., p. 103.
[7] Edward Sapir, 'Language', *Encyclopedia of the Social Sciences*, p. 159.
[8] Melville J. Herskovitz, *Man and His Works* (New York: Knopf, 1948).
[9] Charles Morris, *Signs, Language, and Behavior* (New York: Prentice-Hall, 1946), pp. 35–36.

itself. The skilled radio operator often hears, not letters, but words as audible configurations of long and short whistles.

The extent to which language influences the higher thought processes as they relate to the codification and standardization of man's reaction to his environment is still undetermined. Gardner Murphy holds that language makes distinctions and distinctions make language. Through the medium of language man fragments the world about him into patterns that are meaningful to him, and then combines these patterns in ways that are culturally unique so that members of differing cultures see phenomena in quite differing contexts. Thus language is a matrix into which thought is molded and behavior canalized.[10] Whorf and Sapir agree that human beings are very much at the mercy of the language that has become the medium of expression for their society, and that language is much more than an incidental means for solving specific problems of communication.[11] Niels Bohr has written, 'It is, above all, essential to realize that no proper human thinking is imaginable without the use of concepts framed in some language which every generation has to learn anew.'[12]

But, John Lotz, though he admits that language exerts a powerful influence upon man's psychological behavior and his powers of cognition, asserts that the 'exact rôle of language in thinking and logic is unknown', and the assertion that had Aristotle been a Mexican the logic of the Western World would have been quite different, 'seems to rest on dubious grounds'.[13] Whatmough denies that grammatical categories or large-scale patterning impose compulsion upon action, or that there is any evidence to show that such concepts as time and space have been imposed by language. On the contrary, he insists, language has again and again pointed a way out from restriction on action, and opened the way to new avenues of thought.[14] Finally, Werner Heisenberg has shown the inadequacy of language for the atomic

[10] Gardner Murphy, *Human Potentialities* (New York: Basic Books, 1958), pp. 84–86.

[11] Benjamin Lee Whorf, *Language, Thought, and Reality* (New York: Wiley, 1956), pp. 134 ff.

[12] Niels Bohr, *Atomic Physics and Human Knowledge* (New York: Wiley, 1958), p. 28.

[13] John Lotz, 'Linguistics – Symbols Make Man, in Lynn White, Jr.', *Frontiers of Knowledge* (New York: Harper, 1956), pp. 226–227.

[14] Joshura Whatmough, *Language: a Modern Synthesis* (New York: Mentor, 1957), p. 201.

physicist, who must follow Birkhoff, Neumann, and more recently Weizsacker, in rejecting even the precision of mathematics as an instrument of creative thought. Weizsacker would substitute for conventional modes of expression an extension of classical logic to the point of rejecting the law of *tertium non datur* – a third possibility does not exist. In classical logic there is no alternative to the factual assertions 'here is a table', or 'here is not a table', but modern atomic physics demands a language capable of expressing degree of truth. The difficulties of definition and distinction can be avoided, Heisenberg points out, if one's discourse is confined to facts, i.e., experimental results. But, if one wishes to speak of the atomic particles themselves one must use mathematics as a supplement to vernacular language or 'combine it with a language that makes use of modified logic or no well-defined logic at all'. For 'in the experiments about atomic events we have to do with things and facts, with phenomena that are just as real as any phenomena in daily life. But the atoms, or the elementary particles, themselves are not as real; they form a world of potentialities or possibilities, rather than one of things or facts'.[15]

To the philosopher of language, Heisenberg's argument is something of a double-edged sword, for, while it seems to prove that man's thought can advance beyond the limits of his vernacular language, it cannot advance very far, if at all, without the invention of a new medium of expression by means of which the mind can effectively seize upon concepts, speculations, or other manifestations of the cognitive process. Thus, one can conclude only that not until much more is known than is now available about the nature of knowledge itself, how it is generated, and the manner in which it is transmitted through society, will it be possible to assess with accuracy the rôle of language in human intellectual behavior. We cannot let ourselves forget the cynicism of Mephistopheles' reply to the assertion of the Student that 'in each word some concept there must be' –

> *Quite true! But don't torment yourself anxiously;*
> *For at the point where concepts fail,*
> *At the right time a word is thrust in there.*

[15] Werner Heisenberg, *Physics and Philosophy* (New York: Harper, 1958), pp. 185–186.

> *With words we fitly can our foes assail,*
> *With words a system we prepare,*
> *Words we quite fitly can believe,*
> *Nor from a word a mere iota thieve.*

Thus he concludes:

> *Upon the whole – to words stick fast!*
> *Then through a sure gate you'll at last*
> *Enter the templed hall of Certainty.*

II. LANGUAGE AND LIBRARIANSHIP

Traditionally language has been regarded as a humanistic discipline and the special province of the philologists, grammarians, and linguists. But these groups have concerned themselves with language as a structured inventory of words and the meanings for which the words stand. The great German philologists of the late nineteenth century interpreted the application of science to linguistics as the formulation of laws, principles, and rules of syntactical structure, of word relationships and origins, and of patterns of consonant interchange. Thus they sought the discovery of families of languages and from these derived hypotheses respecting the origins of language itself. Only in such realms as literary criticism and *explication de texte* were they much involved with language as an instrument of communication, and they neglected almost entirely the symbolic character of language and its relationships to the growth of cultures.

In time, linguistics aroused the interest of the logicians who, especially in classical logic, were concerned with syntactic structure, dialectics, and the forms and relationships of the declarative sentence. But the logicians forget that language is a convention that has evolved through centuries of use with little thought for the highly stylized structures of logic, unambiguous connection between premise and deduction, and the simple patterns of reasoning with which the logician must deal. Man employs language in whatever way may meet his immediate needs, and such use can serve to obscure truth as well as to reveal it. The great fault of the logicians in attacking the problems of language is over-simplification. Thus they are compelled to rule out from their narrow world of discourse the obvious fact that almost any word may produce a variety of responses within the human mind. They fail to consider the fact that language can represent some aspects of reality much more accurately than is possible through the use of stylized logical patterns.

Most recently the engineers have begun to explore language, but they, too, have been primarily concerned with its communicative aspects. Moreover, they speak of communication in a very specialized way particularly with reference to theories of signaling, and the forces which contribute to, or detract from, the ability of a given signal, or set of signals, to convey information. Admittedly the engineers have brought a new perspective to the study of language, and they have made a significant contribution to it by demonstrating the potentialities of mathematics as a tool for a better understanding of language as communicated message. But they have not made the transition from signal to symbol, and they have been more concerned with how a message is transmitted than why it has been sent or the socio-psychological impact of the transmission. Language is much more than a vehicle of communication, however thoroughly one may comprehend the engineering of the transmission process.

Thus one arrives at the psychologists and the cultural anthropologists who, in the opinion of the present writer, have more of importance to say for the complete understanding of language than any other single group. For language, in the final analysis, is a product of the human mind, generated in a social context. To be sure, the psychologists will derive much help from the engineers and mathematicians, and this assistance may be expected to increase in the future. Nor can the cultural anthropologists divorce themselves entirely from the study of linguistics. Perhaps Melvil Dewey was right after all in placing Language between Science and Sociology in his classification. But it is in an effective union of psychology and anthropology that one may expect to find the most significant contributions to a better understanding of the nature of language and its relationships to the growth of human knowledge.

With this inter-disciplinary approach to the problem of language and the improvement of communication across geographic and political barriers the library has a very vital interest. By tradition the librarian is concerned with the communication of intellectual and aesthetic values through the medium of graphic

L

records, and to achieve his ends he must be familiar, not only with the processes of communication, but also with the nature of knowledge itself, the manner in which it is generated, and the means by which it is disseminated through society. His task is that of synthesis and in that synthesis all disciplines are fused. This synthesis is in itself an act of creation, the creation of a symbolism by which the results of scholarship can be communicated across whatever barrier man in his fumbling way has erected in the paths of his own progress.

Quite unconsciously perhaps, the librarians have laid the foundations for this newer symbolism. Through the adoption of certain classification systems as standards they have at least begun to make some progress toward a unitary symbolism for the logical structuring of all knowledge. Such unitary symbolism will go far toward facilitating the processes of comprehension, as well as of communication, throughout the entire world of scholarship. Here may be found the beginnings for the transposition of methods and concepts for the interrelating of facts, laws, and theories within and among the disparate fields of thought. The systematization that is born of standardized bibliographic classification makes possible the invention of linguistic analogies, or homomorphic images or concepts among the various areas of scholarship. Thus communication among those who speak different native tongues becomes mainly a problem of devising transposable linguistic forms that stimulate in the minds of scholars of varying national origins and cultures common isomorphic thought patterns. In creating such standardized patterns the taxonomists have, perhaps, had the greatest success within the disciplines that comprise the biological sciences, but the librarians have extended the general acceptance of these patterns over a much broader horizon.

It is, however, in the area of notation, especially in such notational systems as the Universal Decimal and the Colon scheme of Ranganathan, that the librarians have achieved the greatest measure of success in the creation of an international symbolism. This does not imply that these notations have been devised with any great measure of skill or have been used economically. The Colon notation has achieved a degree of refinement that merits respect, particularly when contrasted with the lack of sophistication exhibited by the UDC. But each has been accepted internationally, and each in its primitive way has begun to assume some of the symbolic elements that any medium of universal communication, or discourse, must exhibit. The encoding techniques now being developed at Western Reserve University may well be the foundation of a natural bridge of communication across linguistic barriers, and one of the objectives of this Conference* is to bring to light similar work in progress elsewhere.

III. CRITERIA FOR AN ADEQUATE SYMBOLISM

If language is not to be regarded as an inventory of conventional signs, but a closely woven fabric of interrelated symbols, it follows that any mechanism adequate to the task of promoting standardized communication must provide for three universal aspects of knowledge: (*a*) the dynamic, evolutionary, and functional processes; (*b*) the static and structural features of phenomena; and (*c*) the teleological, or purposive, modes of behavior. To these may be added: (*d*) the temporal which relates to change, growth, and function; (*e*) the spatial which is the characteristic displayed in morphology, structure, isomorphism, and taxonomy;[16] and (*f*) the synthetic or symbolic. The time–space mode however is, in a sense, the differentiating element between the dynamic and the static, and the synthetic is characteristic of the teleological.

A groping toward these modes of knowledge is to be seen in the signs and symbols of association of the Universal Decimal Classification, though they have been stated much more explicitly in Ranganathan's facet formula of time, space, material, energy, and personality. Again, they are inherent in the encoding system, especially in its rôle indicators, devised at Western Reserve. Henry E. Bliss was reaching toward much the same objective when he attempted to synthesize in his scheme an 'order of nature' which was a composite of several sub-orders such as the historical, the developmental, and the pedagogic. Thus it is evident that the librarian has for many years been dealing in

[16] Oliver L. Reiser, *The Integration of Human Knowledge* (Boston: Porter Sargent, 1958), p. 84.

* International Conference for Standards on a Common Language for Machine Searching and Translation, Cleveland, Ohio, September 1959.

symbolism much as Molière's M. Jourdain had been speaking prose.

To the layman, however, coding is usually regarded as a form of symbolism designed for but two purposes, either to conceal the contents of a message from all but those privileged few who possess the key to its meaning, or to economize the communication process by reducing it to a form of short-hand. But this conference is not concerned with the code as a localized substitute for the vernacular, but rather as a symbolic system which brings into coincidence the conceptual pattern of a document, or graphic record, with the conceptual pattern of the person or persons who has recourse to it. Its objective, therefore, is not to conceal the content of a message or to economize in its transcription, but to make it more widely available. Thus the immediate concern of this conference is with symbolism as catalyst. For the symbolism of translation and of information retrieval must be much more than a codification of verbal isolates. The code upon which the symbolism is based must make possible the relation, comparison, and correlation of the thought content of the message in ways that are coincident with the operations of the human brain. It must be able to manipulate both specific and generic concepts and to relate the one to the other. It must operate on several semantic levels, for in human discourse, whether direct or indirect, relations are as vital to meaning as are the intentions of the constituent parts. Therefore structure, pattern, and other manifestations of verbal configuration must be symbolized in the code.

One may, therefore, regard the code, in reality, as a language itself, or to draw a somewhat more precise distinction, a metalanguage, a set, as Morris says, of 'plurasituational signs', capable of both oral and graphic representation with meanings that are unambiguously interpretable to a common culture or subculture. Similarly, the act of coding, like the act of translating, is a process of substituting one set of signs for another while holding the symbolism, or conceptual content of the message, constant. Finally, the process of information retrieval is also a series of acts whereby concepts in the mind of the searcher are brought into coincidence, or near coincidence, with the recorded concepts of graphic records through a medium of conventional and codified symbols the manipulation of which is executed internally by the human brain either with or without the external assistance of a mechanical device. Thus, both translation and information retrieval involve conceptual transfer through a symbolic medium, e.g.:

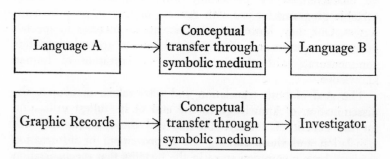

Viewed from the standpoint of the principles involved, whether or not the intermediary transfer point is mechanized is irrelevant: the only requirement is that the act of transfer take place. However, if this conceptual transfer is to be mechanized, whether the aim is translation or information retrieval, the systems for recording knowledge symbolically exhibit certain fundamental or basic characteristics or aspects. The simple fact that both translation and information retrieval require an intermediary agent, a communication bridge, between a body of recorded knowledge and a human mind in search of a message therefrom, and the fact that this intermediary agent, or catalyst, must be expressed in symbolic form means that the mechanical system by which this transfer is to be accomplished must be capable of manipulating this symbolism, or code, in ways that approximate the patterned operations of the human brain. The more nearly exact this approximation the more effective the transfer. To make possible the design of such a code, both for mechanized translation and information retrieval, certain common problems of relational and syntactical interpretation must be solved. Quite possibly these problems must be attacked on more than one level of detail. Both translation and retrieval necessitate a high degree of terminological or lexical control, for without this the symbolism loses much of its discreteness with a resulting excess of redundancy, ambiguity, general confusion, and loss of meaning. This necessitates the achievement of consensus in the solution of common terminological problems, especially those respecting the standardization of meanings and relationships and their symbolic representations in the code, or codes. Finally, in both mechanized translation and mechanized retrieval the system, or systems, should be characterized by potentially interchangeable or interconvertable programs for use with general, or special, purpose computers. One may, however, prognosticate an increase in special-purpose computers and a decrease in the use of general computers commensurate with the increase in specialization of human knowledge.

The goal of both translation and retrieval is, of course, the dissemination of knowledge to the end of its fullest utilization for the benefit of society. To this end those concerned with translation and those seeking the improvement of information retrieval have a common stake in the benefits that mechanization has to offer, an interest that may be theoretical but which always has a pragmatic objective. This Conference, then, is not dedicated to the defense of the machine but only to the co-operative exploration of the advantages that the machine may have to offer in improving the processes of translation and retrieval, and the ways in which those advantages, if they exist, may be exploited.

IV. THE CONFERENCE GOALS

Progress in a number of countries, many of which are represented at these meetings, seems to demonstrate that the problems inherent in the effective use of electronic mechanisms for the translation and retrieval of scientific and technical information can be solved. During recent years a substantial number of institutions, organizations, and government agencies have been directing research and development programs toward the solution of such problems, and though these efforts are widely scattered geographically and though the avenues of communication among them are less than adequate, similar basic principles and techniques are being applied in many explorations. Yet, despite these similarities there is divergence in such procedural features as code design, modes of recording, and language analysis.

Much of this divergence is due, of course, to differences in purpose and circumstances of use, and certainly it is not in itself to be deplored. Nevertheless, no one can rightly deny the advantages of agreement, or at least reasonable unanimity, in establishing objectives and goals, and the contribution which recognized standards for a common machine language can make for ultimate success in solving the total information problem. From a concerted scrutiny of these problems some progress toward acceptable standards and goals should certainly emerge. With this hope in view, then, the specific aims of the conference are six in number:

1. To create an environment favorable to the promotion of a common machine language, or a series of compatible machine languages, for processing scientific and technical literature so that it may be searched, selected, correlated, and translated by means of automatic equipment.

2. To specify equipment requirements and characteristics for use with common language systems or with compatible machine languages.

3. To create an environment that will foster co-operative processing and exchange of encoded materials for machine searching.

4. To promote the co-operative collecting and analysis of scientific and technical terminology for the preparation of code dictionaries and thesauri to be used in machine searching and machine translation.

5. To promote co-operative research programs and encourage and expedite the free exchange of research materials, both nationally and internationally.

6. To review in as great detail as possible the interrelationships between mechanized literature searching and machine translation and to consider how, through an intensified program of research, progress in one field may advance the other.

The environmental aspects of these objectives have been deliberately stressed, for the first important step in the inauguration of such a program as is here envisaged is the creation of a climate of opinion that is hospitable to the free exchange of ideas, plans, programs, and achievements. We cannot, indeed, in these few days solve all the problems that plague the information specialist and create barriers to the extension of human knowledge. But certainly we can identify those problems that most seriously need solution, we can make plans for a co-operative attack upon them, and we can pool our intellectual resources. It is not too much to hope that from this Conference will come other conferences, more extensive co-operative programs of research, and greater research potential than any one of us working alone can command. We are here to direct our attention to some of the fundamental problems of language as, in the broadest sense, it contributes to the dissemination of knowledge among men. Let us, then, use our linguistic capabilities to the fullest possible extent in the mastery of language itself.

As scientists and scholars we may be distrustful of language, for we know that the power of words is not always a benevolent power, it can be used to conceal vast caverns of ignorance and to lead men into the pathway of error. Moreover, we are held in the web of language as if by bands of steel; we cannot escape it. Yet, within language lies our power to 'think things out', from it has derived the vast body of modern science, and without it we could never have created the stupendous artifacts of the modern world. It is the vehicle of all our progress. It is the first concern of the librarian because librarianship itself is basically a science of communication. It is, therefore, especially fitting and proper that a school of library science should co-sponsor such a conference as this, for we are here concerned with problems that lie at the very core of librarianship. I do not exaggerate, nor do I indulge in fanciful speculation, when I express the hope that the results of the deliberations of this conference will greatly enrich the professional equipment of the librarian, and will better prepare him adequately to fulfill his rôle in society.

11: *How Engineers Can Keep Abreast of Professional and Technical Developments*

THE PROBLEM to which I have been asked to address myself – How can engineers keep abreast of professional and technical developments? – recognizes the operation of a kind of Malthusian principle whereby information tends to increase more rapidly than the means for its assimilation. One of the characters of James Thurber states it in terms less doctrinaire: 'So much has already been written about everything,' she says, 'that you can't find out anything about it.' To the paradox of this good Irish bull there are three possible answers. First, one might deny the reality of the exponential growth of human knowledge and, like a modern King Canute, hold back the paper flood by royal decree. Or, one may seek escape through cynicism, and declare with Calvin Mooers that, since ignorance is bliss, it is more painful and troublesome to have information than to do without it, and hence the utility of an information system may be said to vary inversely to its efficiency. One could cite in support of this view the farmer who knew more about farming than he 'ever used'. Finally, one might attempt to attack scientifically the identification of the engineer's reading behavior pattern, but this is perhaps the most discouraging approach of all, for one will not have gone very far before he discovers that there is only very slight evidence to show *why* engineers read, *what* they read, or even whether they *can* read.

NEED OF 'COMMUNICATION'

A recent study conducted by the Operations Research staff of

Presented to the Design Engineering Conference of the American Society of Mechanical Engineers, Chicago, Ill., 1962.

the Case Institute of Technology indicates that chemical engineers spend more time in 'communication' (i.e., reading, talking, and listening) than in any other form of professional activity, including laboratory research. This finding suggests that the *laboratory* may be for *oratory* rather than for *labor*. Though Sir Francis Bacon may have been right that reading does make a full man, the great Sir Francis did not say with what a man is by reading filled. Indeed, if one can accept the results of an inquiry into the ways in which scientists and engineers keep themselves informed made by Scates and Yeomans for the American Council on Education, these two professional groups evinced very little interest in filling their minds with anything. In general, the reading of a very limited number of technical journals was the main avenue for maintaining awareness of scientific advances, though some use was made of conferences and professional meetings as vehicles of scientific communication. But even when one accepts the most generous interpretation of available evidence, one can find little proof that there exists a great yearning for new knowledge.

Prior to the Second World War, and indeed a few years thereafter, studies of sources of scientific information were largely restricted to statistical analyses of citations in scientific publications. Growing dissatisfaction with the limitations of citation analysis brought forth in the late 1940s and during the decade of the 1950s a very substantial quantity of studies, some of which attacked the problems of the reading habits of scientists, while others analyzed the characteristics of abstracting and indexing services, and yet others identified the totality of information sources available and in use in designated subject fields or in particular laboratory or research situations. Interest in these areas of research was greatly stimulated by a number of important conferences, beginning with the historic conference of the Royal Society in 1948 and continued by the conferences on Bibliography in an Age of Science at the University of Illinois and that on Bibliographic Organization at the University of Chicago, both in 1950, a second conference at Chicago in 1952, this time on the communication of scientific information, the conference on the Practical Utilization of Recorded Knowledge at Western Reserve University in 1956, another conference in Cleveland in 1957, and the International Conference on Scientific Information held at

Washington in November 1958. It would not be possible in an essay as brief as this to summarize even the more important studies in a long list that includes among others such names as Bernal, Bradford, Urquhart, Herner, Shaw, Voigt, Fussler, Stevens, and assorted Smiths, Scotts, and Williamses. There have been several excellent surveys of the literature dealing with studies of printed information and its use by scientists, of which the most notable are those by Margaret Egan and Ralph Shaw, both of which were made in 1956, that by Elin Tornudd in 1958, and by Melvin Voigt in 1961.

THE SCIENTIST'S USE OF LITERATURE

From the studies of the scientists' use of literature that have been made over the past twenty years, of which there are approximately seventy-five, it is possible to draw certain generalizations concerning the ways in which scientists use literature to keep abreast of current developments and innovations in their respective fields. First, the reading of scientists and engineers, like that of all other human beings, is strongly influenced by the availability of the material to be read. A scientist may be willing to walk a mile for a Camel, but he won't walk very far for a book; if he's not near the book he'd read, he'll read the book he's near. Therefore, those who seek to improve the ability of the scientist to keep abreast of the literature must first direct their attention to the minimization of this intellectual inertia by improving bibliographic and library services. Moreover, dependence upon recorded information varies with the nature of the scientist's work. Research investigators, teachers in academic institutions, and information specialists comprise the largest groups of library users. They are also the greatest contributors to the stocking of the library's shelves, and one may guess that there is a positive relationship between the reading of books and the writing of them. He who runs may read, but he who writes must jolly well read or he will find himself in deep trouble. By contrast, scientists employed by industry for duties other than research and development have been found to make only very limited use of literature, and in the opinion of many, no group makes as extensive use of recorded information as it should.

USE OF LIBRARY RESOURCES

A direct correlation has also been found between the scientist's educational record and the extent of his use of literature. This finding strongly suggests the importance of courses in subject literature and the use of library resources, especially for those with the lower academic degrees. The absence of skills in the use of information sources is a strong argument for the inclusion of such training in the curricula of science departments and in institutes of technology, yet it has been an area which, with the possible exception of chemistry and biology, has been almost totally ignored.

A limited number of comparative studies indicate that workers in the more exact sciences tend in general to depend more heavily upon the literature of their fields than do the applied scientists and engineers on theirs. Engineers have sought to explain their neglect of recorded knowledge with vague references to the secrecy with which much of applied research is necessarily surrounded, but a more plausible explanation would seem to lie in the engineer's professional training which, in most instances, is not literature oriented. The majority of engineers would still rather pour a ton of concrete or squint through a transit than read a book. Finally, it will come as no surprise to anyone to learn that foreign languages are a serious barrier to the use of scientific literature, especially in the United States where colleges and secondary schools have established such an unenviable record in linguistic education. Mathematics is the mother tongue of the engineer, and one might even add that English is a poor second.

The fortuitous way in which scientists discover the existence of recorded information relevant to their work has been emphasized in a study by Bentley Glass and Sharon Norwood. They found that in almost half (44·6 per cent) of the cases studied, casual conversation and references in journals regularly scanned were the prime sources of the scientist's information about work relevant to his own activity. The remaining 56 per cent was scattered among a wide variety of sources of which abstracts and indexes account for only 6·4 per cent. The authors concluded that the most striking fact revealed by their study was 'unquestionably the very heavy reliance by most workers in nearly every field checked, on verbal communication with scientists working in the same area'.

THE SCIENTIST'S APPROACH TO INFORMATION

To free his data from the restrictive influence of the language bias, at least that was the excuse he used, Melvin J. Voigt spent a year in the Scandinavian countries on a Fulbright grant in 'determining scientists' approaches to information and to relating these approaches to the purposes for which the information was sought'. Perhaps the most important conclusions that can be drawn from his inquiry are: (1) that there is no universally applicable bibliographical instrument or method that will meet all informational requirements and needs; (2) as subjects proliferate and the output of research increases in volume and complexity the standard bibliographic approaches become increasingly inadequate and unsatisfactory; (3) that bibliographic services designed to meet the requirements of exhaustive retrospective bibliographic searching are most likely to succeed if they are internationally based and receive the full co-operation of as many countries as possible, but for current-awareness service international co-operation is much less important and satisfactory; (4) that for current-awareness services, promptness of publication, coverage designed to meet the needs of a well-defined group of users, and ease of use are the characteristics to be emphasized; (5) thorough and informative abstracts are less important for current-awareness services than they are for retrospective searching; (6) there is a surprising degree of uniformity in the information-gathering behavior of scientists working in the same field of specialization and, therefore, bibliographic tools designed to meet the needs of a specific field will find ready acceptance by all scientists working in that field; (7) the most important information problem of the scientist today, regardless of the specialization in which he is engaged, is the need to keep abreast of current developments, and therefore documentalists and librarians should de-emphasize their present concern with retrospective searching and devote greater attention to the development of express information services and other techniques for improving current awareness. Finally, there seems to have been general uncertainty and even apprehension about the future rôle of mechanization in information retrieval. On the one hand, there appeared to be a consensus that the importance of mechanization to information retrieval will increase, but on the other hand, the hope was widely expressed that the advent of the computer in information retrieval could be postponed for several generations. One cannot but wonder whether this aversion to mechanization would be as prevalent among American scientists and engineers as it seems to be among the Scandinavians.

WHAT DO SCIENTISTS AND ENGINEERS READ?

But if we accept the validity of the evidence that scientists and engineers consume more time in communicating than in any other form of professional activity, and that they are averse to the delegation of their prerogatives to stumble about in the literature in their own fumbling ways, such questions naturally arise as: What do scientists and engineers read? What are the purposes for which they read? And what are some of the influences that shape the pattern of their reading? The five-year study conducted by the Operations Research unit at the Case Institute of Technology has contributed some provisional answers. The Case investigators found that, though scientists consume substantial amounts of time in communication, only about 3 per cent of their time is employed in reading scientific journals and any one scientist never reads more than about one-half of one per cent of all the articles published in his field of specialization. This would seem to indicate a serious need for improved means for identifying the really pertinent materials, but there is strong evidence that abstracts do not serve such a function inasmuch as they are generally used as a substitute for the original articles rather than as a subject guide to them. Despite the fact that scientists and engineers spend substantial amounts of time in oral communication, the Case studies revealed that about twice as much time is required, on the average, to transmit one unit of information to one individual orally, as is required to communicate the same amount of information by written means. Time consumed in professional reading was also found to increase in direct proportion to the availability of company libraries and their services. One is scarcely surprised to learn from the Case authorities that the industrial chemist, for example, spends more time in reading than in writing, but it does come as something of a shock to learn that he spends more time talking than listening. Obviously, industrial chemists consume substantial amounts of time talking to themselves, or they talk simultaneously in groups – a kind of chemo-corale or recitative. Chemists in universities, however, where teaching is a major concern, spend twice as much time transmitting information as receiving it. For some teachers we have known this proportion would seem a little low, but judgment would have to rest on the definition of information.

The reading time of the scientists was divided almost equally between browsing (51 per cent) and directed reading for a specific purpose (49 per cent); in both instances the article was the main focus of attention, three-fourths of the reading time being devoted to it by the directed reader, and slightly less than half by the browser. The browser, as one might expect, devoted substantial amounts of time to abstracts, or digests, advertisements, tables of contents, and letters to the editor. Both the motivated reader and the browser expended significant amounts of time, in the case of the former more than 10 per cent, in scrutinizing charts, diagrams, and illustrations. Scientists and engineers, like other human beings, are strongly attracted by pictures.

The very high concentration of the scientists' reading is evident from the fact that fewer than ten journals accounted for more than half of the entire journal reading time, despite the fact that thousands of scientific and engineering journals are published annually. In the end, however, one is forced to recognize that the results of the Case study, despite the care taken in its construction and execution, are not conclusive. In most instances the percentage differentials are so small that any really valid generalizations cannot be drawn from them. The past ten years may have brought some heroic attempts to expose to scientific analysis the reading behavior of scientists, but as the shoemaker's children are traditionally supposed to be unshodden, so the scientist has failed to be very scientific in studying himself.

COMPLEXITY OF ACQUIRING INFORMATION

We are still quite far from any real understanding of how scientists read, why they read as they do, and the ways in which the efficiency of their reading can be improved. That this is true,

I submit, is because the act of reading itself, the mechanism by which we acquire information, is far more complex than has generally been assumed. Because we are habitual readers, whether for pleasure, for profit, or for release from boredom, we have come to take the act of reading, of acquiring information through the medium of the printed page, for granted, and any real understanding of reading must wait upon the researches of the neurologists, the brain specialists, and certain battalions in that heterogeneous army which calls itself psychologists. To the work of these must be added a better understanding of how knowledge is generated and augmented, the ways in which it is disseminated through society, and the impact it has upon social patterns and behavior. This is epistemology, but it is a new kind of epistemology which seeks a deeper understanding of the rôle of scientific knowledge in the totality of the social *milieu*.

Problem Solution Requires Information

The mission of the engineer is the solution of problems, and problem solution requires information, whether that information be acquired directly through personal experience, or vicariously through communication with other individuals or the medium of graphic records. The solution of problems is as old as the history of man, for problems have always been present in man's environment, and from the beginning man has applied to their solution such intelligence as he possessed. But man could not survive as an individual. If he was to reduce the uncertainty of the outcome of his actions, he would be compelled to enlist the collective power of the group in the solving of his environmental problems. Thus the communication of information became the key to organized problem solving, whether the problem to be solved was the preservation of life against the ravages of a common enemy, the building of a new structure, or the discovery and explanation of a natural law.

David Hertz and Albert Rubenstein, in their pioneering study of team or group research, have placed substantial emphasis upon the importance of four types of information essential to the solution of problems either by the individual or by the group – they are conceptual, empirical, procedural, and stimulatory.

Conceptual Information

Conceptual information is composed of ideas, theories, and

hypotheses about the relationships that exist among the particular fields or areas of the problem being investigated, or in the disciplines which in some way may be brought to bear upon it. The sources of conceptual information are very broad; they include the totality of the individual's past experience, all the media of recorded scientific information, and direct personal contact with other workers. The transfer of conceptual information generally requires considerable motivation, and the rate at which it is transferred or assimilated is usually rather low. It may require the formulation of new languages, or modes of expression, even the development of derivative or auxiliary sciences; but because of the time required to generate new conceptual information the communication process itself acts as an effective check on errors in transmission. Conceptual information is the philosophical framework of all research and without it all discovery becomes fortuitous dissociated observation and consciously creative work is impossible.

Empirical Information

Few industrial research and engineering problems can be solved without empirical information, and its source is generally experience in the laboratory or the field. But the literature may also provide a substantial amount of experimental and empirical information, and the need for it is often the justification for the exhaustive literature search. Personal contact is also an important source of empirical information, but because the time required for its discovery and assimilation is usually considerably less than that for conceptual information it does not possess the self-contained safeguards of the latter against errors in transmission. Nevertheless, empirical information provides the stairway by which the scientist may ascend from the foundation theory to the solution of his particular problem, and it must be an important part of the informational intake of every investigator.

Procedural Information

Though there are procedural elements common to many fields of activity, each branch of science and engineering has developed certain types of procedural information that are characteristically its own. The testing, handling, and manipulating of data, the measuring of effectiveness, the construction of hypotheses – all

M

are procedures with their respective bodies of recorded knowledge that must be assimilated into the total informational store of the scientist and engineer. Procedural information is probably the easiest of the four major types to communicate and in its transmission the problem of error is not serious. Nevertheless, the efficiency of problem solving is strongly influenced by the efficiency of the procedures employed, and, therefore, careful attention must be given to this form of research communication.

Stimulatory Information

The last variety of information, stimulatory, is the most difficult of all to define because it relates in an intangible way to the creation of an intellectual atmosphere conducive to research productivity. One might argue that it is essentially environmental rather than communicative, nevertheless communication has an important part in it. Attendance at professional meetings, opportunity to publish, participation in informal social activity, all of these generate and foster stimulatory information that incites scientific curiosity.

Because Hertz and Rubenstein are primarily concerned with team research they have added two additional types of information, those relating to *policy* and *direction*, and the importance of both to co-ordinated group activity is certainly not to be minimized. We can, however, dismiss them here with only brief mention because our primary concern is with the scientist working as an individual. Nevertheless, the individual must have some need for an awareness of institutional policy and direction, and with the increase in the volume and complexity of knowledge and the growing importance of the interdisciplinary attack upon scientific problems, one can quite properly surmise that team research will assume greater and greater importance in the work of the scientist, and that increasingly he will be required to adjust his methods of operation to the collective demands of the group.

CONCLUSION

These several kinds of information are not isolated or independent strands in the communication network; they are overlapping, concurrent, and highly interdependent. The pattern into which they are woven is intricate, infinitely variable, and only imperfectly envisaged and understood. But the comprehension of the communication process and the largely unanswered question of the ways in which the engineer can best keep up with the output of new research that is relevant to his interest are not mere academic excursions undertaken for the experience of the journey, nor do they pose problems that are of concern only to the dean of a library school who is in search of expanding markets for the products of his classrooms. Information and its effective communication constitute a great national resource, and its husbandry is a matter for national concern.

In a report on 'The Sources of Economic Growth in the United States', recently prepared for the Committee on Economic Development by its associate director of research, Edward F. Denison, the point is made that economic growth is very far from being exponential or self-generating. One cannot assume, Denison observes, that the pool of unused technological knowledge will automatically generate dramatic new growth possibilities. Despite mounting expenditures for research and development, technological improvement is becoming increasingly difficult for the heavily industrialized United States to achieve. Research, of course, fosters more research, and invention begets invention, but the real barrier to the acceleration of technological knowledge is, Denison believes, the time required for one advance to lead to another. This time lag, in the opinion of the CED investigator, cannot be appreciably reduced by increasing the amount of money invested in research or the number of people engaged in its pursuit. Thus the big question remains: To what degree will improvement in the communication of scientific information contribute to the reduction of this time lag and the increase in national productivity? This is the one great overriding question to the solution of which those of us engaged in improving the availability of recorded knowledge must dedicate ourselves – probably for the remainder of our professional lives.

12: *Automation and the Reference Librarian*

THE AUTOMATION of libraries through the use of computers and book-finding robots is 'pure fantasy'. Such was the charge brought by John R. Pierce, Director of Communications Research at the Bell Telephone Laboratories, against mechanized information retrieval when he delivered the major address at the dedication of the new John Crerar Library at the Illinois Institutes of Technology. The 'father of the Telstar communications satellite' insisted, according to a report in the *Chicago Sun-Times* for April 4, 1963, that computers are too 'stupid to function in the complex interplay of language and thinking involved in the search for documents. Moreover, even if an information retrieval machine could be invented . . . it would tend to swamp the user under a flood of information he didn't want or couldn't use.' This distinguished scientist believed that 'realistically there ought to be ways of transmitting information contained in many heavy volumes without physically shipping them to people who can't get to libraries but want to do research. One method might be to send the information by wire and reproduce it at a number of places by automatic typewriters.' However, in his opinion 'we have not reached the stage of electronic development at which this seems practical'.[1] Dr Pierce issued his warning against

[1] The Massachusetts Institute of Technology has recently announced the successful operation of a pilot service by which some forty teletypewriters are linked by cable to two computers. Inquiries teletyped from remote parts of the country will be transmitted directly to the computers and the responses returned almost instantaneously. Time-lags result only when the capacity of the computers is exceeded by the volume of incoming questions, and in such situations the questions are stored in the computer and answered in sequence of receipt. Professor Robert M. Fano, who is in charge of the project, has announced that the system will shortly be incorporated in the Teletypewriter Exchange Service (TWX) and thus be available to the entire nation. Already successful tests have been made between MIT and the Systems Development Corporation of Santa Monica, California.

Originally published in *Reference Services Quarterly*, Vol. 3 (July 1964), pp. 3–7.

automation 'deliberately, in order to counteract the sadly fanciful picture that has been painted by some irresponsible people'. According to the *Sun-Times* reporter, 'the veteran staff of librarians' of the Crerar Library 'seconded Pierce's remarks' and found his words 'reassuring'. We doubt not that they did.

Neither do we doubt that there are people (indeed, we have known some of them only too well) who have made and are making irresponsible and glorious prognostications about the mechanization of the library, just as there are those at the other extreme who maintain that the library will remain self-quarantined for ever from a technological movement that is beginning to penetrate almost every form of human activity and has generated a multi-billion dollar industry. Libraries have already been touched by automation in a variety of ways, and the fact that no one has yet installed an electronic computer behind the reference desk does not mean that automation will never contribute to strengthening the services of the reference department. Not many years have passed since a proposal for the bouncing of television sound and pictures off a man-made satellite would have been regarded as visionary, irresponsible, and impracticable.

The speaker at the Crerar dedication challenged the utility of computers and computer-like mechanisms in information retrieval on the grounds that such devices 'have no judgment', and that 'so far no one has been able to devise a so-called thinking machine that has'. Yet, in a recent report to the Council for the Study of Democratic Institutions, Donald N. Michael cites the work of Norbert Wiener and Frank Rosenblatt in constructing machines that teach themselves to make generalizations about the information with which they are stored. Michael concludes, 'It is no fantasy, then, to be concerned with the implications of thinking machines. There is every reason to believe that within the next two decades machines will be available outside the laboratory that will do a credible job of original thinkings, certainly as good thinking as that expected of most middle-level people who are supposed to "use their minds". There is no basis for knowing where this process will stop, nor, as Wiener has pointed out, is there any comfort in the assertion that, since man built the machine, he will always be smarter or more capable than it is.'[2]

[2] Donald N. Michael, *Cybernetics, the Silent Conquest* (Santa Barbara, California: Center for the Study of Democratic Institutions, 1962), p. 9.

But whatever these explorations and prognostications may portend for the shape of things to come, the fact remains that the reference librarian is already beginning to feel the influence of automation, though in most instances the impact is a ricochet rather than a direct encounter. Much of the drudgery and delay in making available large and elaborate collections of scientific and sociological data, such as the recent volumes of the *Applied Mathematics Series* of the National Bureau of Standards, and the publications of the U.S. Bureau of the Census, has been eliminated by automation. Experimentation is also going forward in the application of the computer to typesetting and printing, such as the work of Michael P. Barnett and his associates at MIT in combining the computer with the Photon. Computer composition was employed in preparing the working papers for the 1963 conference of the American Documentation Institute.

Many of the tools long familiar to the reference librarian are now being produced by automated methods. The production of a concordance, which until very recently was properly regarded as demanding a lifetime of devoted effort, can now be accomplished by computer in the space of no more than a few weeks or months. Earlier techniques in subject analysis are being revived by these new mechanical methods, the only significant difference being that mechanization makes possible greater depth of analysis and an increased speed of production. Thus the Key Word in Contest (KWIC) index (which is really concordance indexing), that made its first general debut in *Chemical Titles* and which has so swept the world of documentation that it is being employed even in such fields of bibliographic endeavor as history and the other social sciences, is no more than a derivative of the German *schlagwort*, or catch-title subject catalog or a return to the principles of indexing enunciated by Crestadoro or of Poole's periodical indexing methods. The computer has also played an important rôle in easing the burden and reducing the cost of the citation index introduced by Eugene Garfield. Publishers and a recent doctoral dissertation by Artandi have also been testing the efficiency of the computer for the preparation of conventional book indexes. Attempts, especially those by IBM, to produce conventional abstracts by computer have not as yet been conspicuously successful, but there is little reason to doubt that a defined procedure that will be economical and yet yield satisfactory results will eventually be accomplished. Thus, in many ways, the application of computer and allied technologies are beginning to contribute to the fabrication of conventional reference tools. The preparation of library book catalogs by computer, on the other hand, is now being practiced in many places, and there are those who believe that within little more than a decade or two, the card catalog, which at the turn of the century seemed to be the perfect inventory of the library's store, will be obsolete. That such an innovation would go far to relieve the age-long contest between the reference department and the catalog department for the location in the library building of the bibliography collection is relatively unimportant; far more significant is the obvious fact that a catalog compiled by computer will greatly facilitate the preparation of highly specialized bibliographies, thus materially increasing the resources of all subject departments and the general reference libraries.

The popular conception of automation as applied to the work of the reference librarian suggests a mechanical marvel from which accurate and authoritative answers to questions will be disgorged in immediate response to a push of the proper button. It is true that one class of automational mechanisms is composed of these devices which perform conventional sensing and motor tasks by replacing or improving upon human physical capabilities for executing these same functions and movements. Thus thermostats control automatically the temperature of our houses, mechanical fingers feed sheets of paper into giant printing presses, and one computer can command a battery of lathes, each of which, in an earlier day, required its own operator. But for the reference librarian, a far more significant class of machines is that composed of computers and computer-like devices that perform, at an astonishingly high rate of speed, complex operations from simple counting to the most intricate mathematical, logical, and decision-making operations that are far beyond the limits of man's mental capabilities to perform with equal efficiency and effectiveness if, indeed, he can perform them at all. This latter class, as John Diebold has indicated, now makes it possible and practicable to think of the entire information-handling process as an integrated *system* rather than as a series or continuum of individual steps.[3]

---

[3] John Diebold, *Automation; Its Impact on Business and Labor* (Planning Pamphlet no. 106) (Washington, D.C.: National Planning Association, 1959), p. 3.

To illustrate the differences between these two classes of machines (the imitative and the projective), Michael uses the example of the automated construction of a brick dwelling. The imitative type of automation would imply the invention of an automatic bricklayer, the second projects the designing of a building that would eliminate the laying of bricks. Another illustration would be the transition from the music-making machines (of which the player-piano is one), which imitated the motions of the musician to the modern high-fidelity phonograph, which derived from an analysis of the nature of sound and its impact upon the physiology of the human nervous system. Or, again, one might cite the inventors of the automobile, who did not seek to produce an automated mechanical horse by putting an internal combustion engine on legs to which it would be attached by a system of levers. The potentialities of automation can free the reference librarian from the popular concept of a mechanical stack-boy or the mechanization of a conventional index or process, and permit the librarian to rethink the entire reference procedure as an integrated information system restructured to take the fullest possible advantage of these new electronic tools.

Today, computerized automatic catalog, directory, or dictionary look-up, often dignified by the term 'information retrieval', is a reality – indeed, it was demonstrated for better or worse in the *Library 21* exhibit at the Seattle World's Fair; and, though one can easily demonstrate its accomplishment, its economic justification still remains to be established. Although the first fruits of invention are seldom economically practicable or even rational, there are always a few intrepid souls who will blunder ahead despite warnings from the John Pierces who insist that the impossible is being attempted; and it is well that this is so.

The advent of a push-button library, though it may strike terror to the hearts of those concerned over technological unemployment and human obsolescence, is nevertheless appealing to the imagination, and the improvements that it can bring to the efficient generation of the conventional tools of the professional behind the reference desk have immediate practicality. But the really great promise of automation is to be sought in its projective aspects – the opportunity it affords to analyze the reference process and redefine reference service. The work of the reference librarian has always been dominated by the 'spot question' and the quick answer. This 'hit and run' technique is used for a great deal of the reference librarian's work, and is important in all kinds of library situations. The ready-reference skill of an experienced librarian is something to be greatly admired and probably always will be needed. Any improvements in the compilation and production of better quick-reference tools which can be the result of automation will be worthwhile.

However, as libraries and information both have become more specialized, this 'hit and run' technique often is not enough; yet the pressure of time, the limitation on manpower, the subject inadequacy of the reference librarian's training, the poverty of the tools with which he must work, his inability or unwillingness to look beyond the immediate tasks toward a larger concept of service, has led his patrons, often, but not always correctly, to assume that he was incapable of being anything other than a somewhat superior automaton who could fetch and carry in response to the simpler commands. As a consequence, the responsibility for serious information searching and mastery of the sources of recorded information has remained either with the patron or been transferred to the hands of the 'information scientist' or the subject specialist, hands that were assumed to be more competent and qualified.

The conviction that automation can raise the intellectual level of the reference librarian does not imply a belief that a machine can make a literature specialist out of a simple button-pusher. The fullest utilization of the potential of automation does necessitate a thorough study of the total reference process from the problem that prompts the asking of a question to the evaluation of the response – for the very simple and obvious reason that machine simulation of that process cannot be accomplished without an understanding of the process itself. The symbiotic relationships between men and machines, as described by Norbert Wiener and other cyberneticians, has focused attention on the reference librarian as an immensely intricate organic mechanism, the operation of which is still very imperfectly understood, operating in an information system that is far more complex than has generally been acknowledged.

Any experienced reference librarian can supply a long list of examples of stupid or improperly asked questions that have come across his desk, or entertain a listener for hours with stories of serendipity; but few people have ever stopped to wonder, much less investigate, the relevance of these experiences for the under-standing of the reference process. The documentalists have been more aware than the conventional, not to say tradition-bound, reference librarian of the importance of analyzing objectively the totality of the reference situation, but regrettably they have not drawn upon the wealth of experience of the reference librarian for the basic data of their inquiries. Consequently, neither group has really come to grips with the reference problem. Neither the reference librarians nor the documentalists have attempted to build a bridge of communication to the other, but until there is just such a bond of understanding, any fundamental solution to the problems of reference service will be lost in a welter of emotional argument over the alleged virtues and inadequacies of the machine. Similarly, the results of the ASTIA Reference Test[4] of more than a decade ago, were rejected as they properly should have been; but there is little evidence that we have learned very much from its mistakes. As the refinement of the modern high-fidelity phonograph was dependent not only upon improve-ments in electronics but also upon a better understanding of the physics of sound and the biological processes of hearing, so automation in reference work is not to be interpreted only in terms of electrical circuitry but also through an understanding of the act of human interrogation and its response.

A mechanized reference service is based upon the supposition of the use of an electronic computer-like device in the memory of which is stored a vast quantity of bibliographic or other data from which relevant portions are disgorged in response to a properly programmed search. Thus one must come to think of automated reference work not only in terms of the magnitude of the store, the discriminating power of the system, the ability of the machine itself to compare, correlate, and match, and the speed with which it can perform its selective, or retrieval, operations, but also of the machine in its intellectual setting (the environment of the problem), the relation between the human being and the machine, the economics involved, and above all, the utility of the result. The important point is, and the one that Mr Pierce has completely

---

[4] C. D. Gull, 'Posting for the Uniterm System of Co-ordinate Indexing'. *American Documentation*, Vol. 7 (January 1956), pp. 9–21.

missed, that the machine problems *per se* are well on the way to solution; the great unsolved problems are those which are fundamental to the reference situation itself. In short, we can now build the machines that Mr Pierce says are impossible, but we do not know how to use them intelligently in the reference library environment. The machines are ready for us, or very soon will be, but we are still very far from being ready for machines. When the 'veteran staff' of the Crerar Library 'seconded Pierce's remarks', they were only saying, in effect, that they did not want to face up to the basic problem that machines present.

A reference search, whether it is conducted with the aid of a machine or not, is a composite of many elements. Underlying all is, of course, the information need itself – the motivational source for the formulation of a question which is the verbalized statement of the need. The degree of coincidence between need and question depends upon the skill of the questioner in comprehending his requirements and expressing them in a way that is meaningful to the librarian. Comprehension and communication are the first links in the procedural chain where the search can go astray; for, as every experienced reference librarian knows only too well, the two are very far from being identical, and the results of a search can be completely relevant to an inquiry without being pertinent to the inquirer's need. Once the true target has been understood and communicated, the next step is translation, or conversion, into the language of the system; whether this be a computer code or the subject entries in a bibliography or reference compilation does not alter the fundamental theory of the situation. This, too, is a communication process that is linguistically, or symbolically, based. Expressed somewhat more simply, then, this phase of the operation is a matching of the question, converted when necessary to the language of the system, with the information contained in the store in order to select those materials (that information) most likely to be pertinent to the inquirer's need. Thus, the reference process is a complex associative series of linkages, or events, that progresses from the need to the questioner – to the question – to its interpretation and translation into the language of the system – to the actual search – to the evaluation of the response. Fragmented into its constituent elements the reference process may be graphically presented thus:

NEED – INQUIRER – INQUIRY – LIBRARIAN – SEARCH
(question)

STRATEGY – INFORMATION STORE – SEARCH –
ANSWER – EVALUATION.

The variables in such a communication flow are self-evident. The environment of the question is defined by the characteristics of the need, the questioner's interpretation of that need and his ability to verbalize his desires, the volume of reading he is prepared to do, the amount of time he is willing to devote to this particular question, and his ability to interpret and utilize the results of the search. The search itself is shaped by the ability of the librarian to interpret accurately the request and the need that prompted it, his skill in expressing the inquiry in terms of the characteristics of the system, his search strategy, and his capacity to evaluate the results (output) in terms of its pertinence to the need and relevance to the question asked. Here it should be emphasized that the pertinence of the output is the real concern of the inquirer, but it is the relevance of that output by which the efficiency of the system is to be judged. If the inquiry does not accurately reflect the need, the system may produce results that are completely relevant but not at all pertinent, yet still be a highly effective system. Thus one is brought to a consideration of the characteristics and capabilities of the retrieval system itself: the depth of analysis that it is capable of providing, the language employed by it in relation to the language (or vocabulary) used and understood by the inquirer and the librarian, and the system's discriminating power (the fineness of mesh, so to speak) with which the system makes possible refinements in correlation, association, and synthesis. The complexity of the reference process is apparent from the following chart of its component elements.

One must repeatedly emphasize that the introduction of automation into reference procedures has nothing to do with the configuration of the reference system or the interaction of the subordinate processes of which it is composed. Documentalists turned to the machine as a means for improving the efficiency of the engineering aspects of librarianship. Whether that efficiency can be expressed in savings of time and money will eventually be

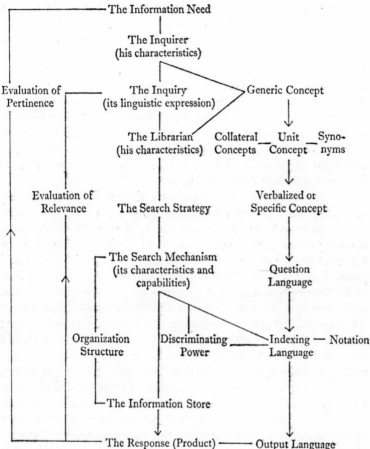

determined by systems analysis and experimentation that will provide reliable data. At the present time the advantages claimed for computers in information retrieval (reference work and bibliographic search) have been neither proved nor disproved. Adequate insight into the component elements of the reference system *qua* system, is still lacking, and the variables that characterize those elements and their relationships to each other are as yet only imperfectly understood. In short, the nature of the tasks that the computer is being asked to perform are not clearly known. As a result of improved insight into the nature of the *indexing* language and the *question* language, computers have become useful in the mapping of associations and the matching of the pattern of the organization of recorded knowledge to the pattern of recourse to that knowledge. The real issue in the automation of reference work is the exploration of the relative effectiveness of conventional and non-conventional reference systems, but the term *non-conventional* is not to be equated with *mechanical* or *electronic*. Admittedly, an intelligent reference librarian equipped with nothing more than the *Bible*, *Shakespeare*, the *World Almanac*, and the *Britannica* is a good match for the most powerful computer and a whole cabinet of interchangeable programs, but such a rhetorical observation does not invalidate the proper rôle of automation in reference service.

The advent of mechanization in the library, if it does nothing more, has been justified by encouraging a few students of the library process to break through the hard crust of conventional thinking about library operations, thus forcing an awareness of the total library system as a configuration of closely interrelated parts. A new understanding of librarianship may eventually prove to be the greatest single gift of automation to the library world, and whether there is in the future a push-button library may now be regarded as almost irrelevant. Plato has cautioned against mistaking shadows for reality, Aesop has warned that one should not risk the loss of that which one has by grasping too greedily and impetuously at its reflection, and Mr Pierce would lull librarians into contentment by insisting that the bright new world is no more than a mirage. All of this is doubtless very good advice in its proper place and time, but one must not forget that there are mirages that are nothing but pure fantasy, but there are also those which reflect a true and accurate image of what lies beyond the horizon, and which will prove to be reliable guides if one has the courage and perseverance to follow where they lead.

13: *The Recruiting of Technical Information Personnel*

TO THE International Conference on Scientific Information held in Washington, D.C., in November of 1958, George S. Bonn of the New York Public Library, presented the most comprehensive survey yet available of facilities for training in scientific documentation.[1] Herman Henkle of the John Crerar Library has prepared for this symposium* a statement which supplements the Bonn report and brings up to date our knowledge of course offerings in library schools for the professional education of technical information personnel. Therefore, this paper will be restricted to the problem of recruiting candidates for careers in technical information.

I believe that the technical information specialist is a variety of librarian, and that he will do his job better if he comes to the field with: (1) a good general education; (2) a measure of subject specialization in the field he proposes to serve; and (3) graduate study in librarianship. But there are those who maintain, with some heat, that library education is so stereotyped, so tradition-bound, that it constitutes a handicap rather than an asset to the initiate. Fundamentally, then, the recruitment of technical information personnel is handicapped by our uncertainty as to the precise nature of the profession, the kind of people who should be brought to it, and the nature of the education the initiates should receive. Such uncertainties are not disastrous but their clarification would materially mitigate the problems of recruitment.

---

[1] George S. Bonn, 'Training for Activity in Scientific Documentation', *Proceedings of the International Conference on Scientific Information*, Vol. 2, (Washington, D.C.:National Academy of Sciences – National Research Council, 1959), pp. 1441–1488.

* Symposium sponsored by the National Science Foundation on the Training of Technical Information Personnel, New York City, April 28–29, 1960. Not previously published.

The recruiting of technical information specialists has been handicapped by the cumulative effect of a variety of circumstances and conditions, most (if not all) of which derive from the youth of the profession. Antecedents of the technical information specialist can doubtless be traced back until they are shrouded in the dim mists of the historic past, but one may reasonably assume that it was the Second World War, and the demands which it brought for a highly developed system of interlocking intelligence operations, that gave the information specialist his first real prominence. With the scientific explosion that followed the surrender of Germany and Japan, and the resultant proliferation of scientific documentation, the work of the information specialist became firmly established as essential to the research activities of business, industry, education, and government; and his rôle has increased in importance during the decade of the fifties.

But because the profession is so young, it has never defined the parameters of its own discipline. As a result, information specialists may be found abstracting, indexing, searching, editing, translating, and performing a variety of miscellaneous duties associated with the organization, retrieval, and dissemination of recorded information within the organizations they happen to serve. This widespread uncertainty as to what the information specialist is supposed to do has quite naturally led to disagreement respecting the kind of person he should be and the nature of the educational program by which he should be trained. Small wonder, then, that heated argument has been prevalent over whether this new activity is a science or an art, whether it is best learned in the classroom or 'on the job', and even whether it is actually a profession or only a genteel technology. Resolution of these questions has not been aided by the obvious fact that successful information specialists have come from quite different educational backgrounds, so that almost any statement that one can make about the educational prerequisites of the information specialist can be countered with an example that conspicuously disproves it. To say, for example, that the technical information specialist should come to his profession through the discipline of the sciences would seem to be a truism, were it not for the fact that those recruited from the humanities are doing their jobs very well indeed – which is not surprising, since the utilization of technical information is basically a communication process, and language, the basis of communication, has long been a humanistic study.

To many, librarianship is a tarnished word, and though this antipathy is slowly passing, there are those (particularly among the scientists) who regard the profession as a form of refined mediocrity. And whether he regards himself as a librarian or not, the technical information specialist shares the stigma of the breed. If, on the other hand, he is regarded as a scientist who 'couldn't make the grade', it may be because sometimes he is. If those who *can* – do, and those who *can't* – teach, then those who *can't teach* – enter librarianship. If technical information is to be made attractive as a specialty, it must establish its professional respectability, it must raise the requirements for admission, and it must demand higher standards of performance. This may sound like asking us to raise ourselves by our own boot-straps, but it is the procedure that every profession has had to follow, for ultimately, professional standards must come from within; they cannot successfully be imposed from without. Respectability, like charity, begins at home.

Acquiring an education has become increasingly expensive, yet despite steeply rising tuition, education continues to be very far from self-supporting. As President Kirk of Columbia University has asked, where but in education can one purchase a commodity or service for less than the cost of its production? Yet all would agree that education should be the reward of those best qualified to profit from it, not those with the ability to pay for it. Professional education for technical information specialists desperately needs financial support, for both programs of research and assistance to students. When the Russians shot their Sputniks into space, they elevated science to new heights of popularity. Medical research has always had tremendous popular appeal. Yet neither physical nor biological science can progress to its fullest potentiality if it is handicapped by inadequate systems for the communication of information. Not until the rôle of the technical information specialist is viewed in its proper perspective, as an integral part of scientific progress, will it cease to be taken for granted and starved with a bare minimum of financial support. So long as scientific documentation must wage a struggle for even a small fragment of the scientific dollar, it will recruit to its ranks only the most dedicated and the most stupid; documentation

N

today cannot compete for personnel with the scientific disciplines dependent upon it. There may be more glamour in a retort than in a tray of edge-notched punched cards, but society must recognize their equality before the bar of scientific advance, and distribute its resources more equitably than it has done in the past.

The very barriers that exist to the effective recruiting of competent people suggest certain remedial measures which must be taken if we are not to accept mediocrity. Most basic of all is the need to put our own house in order – to achieve some measure of agreement respecting the character of the field itself, the nature of the duties to be performed, the kinds of training which best prepare the individual for their performance, and the quality and qualifications of the personnel we wish to attract to it. Fundamentally, this is a problem in definition in the broadest sense.

Secondly, there is the task of interpretation, for the rôle of the technical information specialist must be understood by the community. Both the world of science and the lay public, through an active and well-directed program of public relations, must be made aware of what the information specialist does and the importance of his responsibilities to the advance of human knowledge and the elevation of the standard of living. We may not need to 'glamorize' the profession, but certainly students at both collegiate and secondary school levels should be informed of the intellectual opportunities represented by careers in information handling. There must be more effective liaison than now exists between documentalists and vocational advisors and others who are in a position to direct into the profession students who show promise of superiority in such a field as scientific librarianship. Here, one should observe, is a particularly rich opportunity to enlist the interest of young women who have an aptitude in science but who, because science is dominantly a man's world, have little opportunity for distinction in research careers.

The third area of attack is financial. If able recruits are to be brought to the profession of servicing technical information, the rewards must be economic as well as intellectual. Either alone is insufficient. The fields of chemistry, physics, mathematics, medicine, are all relatively rich in scholarships, fellowships, internships, and grants-in-aid. The writer has been informed recently that not a single graduate student in the department of physics at the University of Chicago or Western Reserve University is paying for his education from his own funds, and probably a similar situation exists in other institutions of higher learning. The present modest resources at the disposal of agencies for the training of librarians (including documentalists) are totally inadequate to meet such competition. Financial support is, however, becoming recognized as a responsibility of industry, business, philanthropic foundations, and government, as well as of the individual student, for those institutions will, in the end, harvest the richest rewards from the work of skilled practitioners. Some subsidization has been direct, through grants for scholarships, fellowships, and loans; some aid has come indirectly, through work-study programs of contract research. However, the resources still lag far behind the need.

Definition, interpretation, and implementation – determining what our needs are, promoting an awareness of those needs, and promoting the means by which the needs can be met – these are the lines of attack which must be followed if superior young men and women are to be brought into the technical information services. If this symposium can lay the foundation for agreement upon the strategy such an attack should follow, it will have made a great contribution, indeed, toward the more efficient use of the scientific knowledge of mankind.

14: *The Library as an Agency of Social Communication*

THE ACT OF communicating is, by definition, the transmission of a message from a communicator to a receptor. The message may be a simple signal or an extensive body of oral or recorded symbolic or pictorial representations. Communication can take place within an individual organism, between two indivduals, or among the members of an aggregate, but always there is a mutually intelligible 'language' as well as a carrier or medium; and while there may be multiple receptors, in any given instance there can be only one transmitter. Just as in the biological organism there is a neural communication system, so in organized societies there is a social communication network. While the agencies which are a part of this network are easily recognized, and their functions easily identified, the fundamental nature of the communication process within society is only imperfectly understood. Students of society know lamentably little about the ways in which knowledge and information are communicated within a culture, even a primitive culture. For that matter, psychologists and specialists in the operation of the human nervous system know precious little about the communication of information within the individual. Analogies have been drawn with the electronic circuitry of the computer just as the communication of information within a society has been likened to the spread of epidemics in a population.

A society is, of course, an aggregate of individuals held together by a complex of cultural and institutional bonds. A society can scarcely know what is not known by any of its members, though the sum of that knowledge may induce in the actions of the group behaviour patterns that differ markedly from those of the individ-

Originally published in *The Journal of Documentation* Vol. 21. no. 4 December 1965

uals that compose it. The study of the ways in which a society achieves an understanding relationship with its environment is what Margaret Egan called 'social epistemology', and it is fundamental to a theory of librarianship.

Graphic records are both an extension of and a check upon the accuracy of the human mind. They are, in the terminology of the semanticist, 'time binders' which span the temporal and spacial distances of our three-dimensional world. The document is an extension of the human powers of communication, and the library is a means for extending the life-span of the document. Like all other social agencies, it has arisen from, and is shaped and re-shaped, according to social necessity. Thus, as graphic records came into being in response to the need of society for a medium that would communicate messages essential to the operation of the social structure, to religious doctrine or ritual, or to any other activity in which the members of the society might engage, so there arose the demand for an agency to control such of those records as needed, for any reason whatever, to be preserved. From the very beginning, libraries have always been an integral part of the 'business' of operating a society, hence a legitimate collective concern.[1] As the culture matured and became more sophisticated, its dependence upon graphic records increased, and changes in the culture were reflected in the librarian's responsibilities.

The librarians of the great collection at Alexandria were much more than mere keepers of the papyrus rolls. They were scholars who studied the texts in their care, participated in the educational and religious activities of their society, and in a variety of ways were an influential force in the total communication system. The medieval libraries and the libraries of the Renaissance did not basically alter these original functions, they only directed them into different channels, again according to their respective social milieus. The invention of printing and the rise of scientific enquiry broadened and increased the importance of the librarian's rôle. Not only did

---

[1] Parenthetically, one should mention that over the centuries libraries have served as symbols of social position, and that their possession or endowment has long been a mark of status. Such recognition of the library is in itself evidence of the value that society places upon it, even though the prestige the library could confer upon its donor had no more to do with its effectiveness as an agency of communication than does the possession today of an expensive automobile relate to the motor car as a means of transportation.

books become more plentiful than they had been during the centuries before Gutenberg, but also the libraries in which they were housed were in a very real sense the laboratories of the scientists. From the seventeenth century to the beginning of modern times, the scientist had only the most meagre of apparatus with which to conduct his investigations. He found it necessary, therefore, to turn to the writings of his predecessors as the most important single source of the knowledge that he needed.

The invention of printing released the bonds that had so firmly restricted knowledge to the privileged few, and made possible, during the nineteenth century, the realization of the American dream of universal education. The emergence of local library societies in the towns of New England and elsewhere along the Atlantic Coast, the growth of the public library, and the rise of academic libraries were tributaries that fed the rich stream of social communication, and gave strength to the democratic movement in the formative decades of the United States.

The complex communication system that operates today in the Western World depends upon many instrumentalities, of which the library is but one. One need not dwell upon the impact that the telegraph, the telephone, the radio and television, not to mention the newspaper and the periodical, have made upon the communication patterns of our society. Each of these has had its effect upon the rôle of the library. With them has come a new urge on the part of the librarian to assume a vigorously active rôle in communication. Librarians no longer are content to accumulate materials in anticipation of use, but seek to engage actively in bringing their resources to the attention of those who need them. The growing importance of all types of graphic records to the successful operation of contemporary society, conditioned as it is by and to science and technology, has forced the librarian to search for and adopt new methods and techniques for making recorded information available not only to scholars but also to business, industry, and government. Effective use of the library has been demanded by the educational system, for elementary and secondary schools as well as institutions of higher learning. In recent years the introduction of automation into a variety of learning and teaching activities has provided the librarian with potentially powerful tools for increasing his effectiveness as a communicator, though the capabilities of these developments have not yet been fully realized.

Over the centuries library techniques and procedures have evolved only slowly and pragmatically, in response to assumed needs and patterned upon *ad hoc* methods. Only rarely have librarians thought seriously of their libraries as social agencies; as Douglas Foskett has said, they have failed to give 'serious consideration to the rôle of libraries (not merely public libraries) in a society, and how the professional community as a whole can best serve society as a whole'.[1] This is very true, but it may not be entirely the librarians' fault if they have nothing to draw on for their practice but unvalidated assumptions—not to say guesses—about the ways in which individuals and societies acquire knowledge and the networks by which knowledge is disseminated. What happens within that psycho-physiological process that take place when a human mind confronts a library store or the bibliographic tools that are intended to be the key to it? How does the knowledge that the individual assimilates become a part of the collective intelligence of a culture? How is social behaviour influenced by the knowledge that society absorbs? These are the basic problems that confront the librarian and should guide his professional practice. Obviously, librarians cannot seek unaided the answers to such questions; they must enlist the help of many specialists in many disciplines. Furthermore, they can, and must, apply the work of others to their own *Weltanschauung*. In the largest sense, the proper study of librarianship is man.

[1] Foskett, D. J., *Science, humanism, and libraries*. London, Crosby Lockwood, New York, Hafner, 1964, p. 239

Index

ABERDEEN Proving Ground, 101
Abstracts, 32, 35, 98, 148
  and literature surveys, 43
  mechanization, 82
  telegraphic, 103
  use of by scientists, 150
Accessibility
  contents, 41
  of information, 50
  physical, 40
Achard, C. F., 59
Adams, Henry, 70
Afcin, 88
Age of Enlightenment, 28
Aitchison, T. M., *xix*
Alberti, Leone Battista, 56
Alexandria, 55, 71, 114, 175
American Chemical Society, 7, 11
American Council on Education, 148
American Diabetes Association, 101
American Documentation Institute
  and ALA, 33
  conference 1963, 160
  and FID, 5
  and SLA, 33
American Library Association, 25, 33
American Society for Metals, 101
American Society of Mechanical
  Engineers, 7, 147
Ampère, André Marie, 58
Aquinas, St Thomas, 79
Archives, 27
Arendt, Hannah, 134
Aristotle, 55, 58, 136
Arizona, University of, 101
Armed Services Technical Informa-
  tion Agency (ASTIA), 164
Artandi, Susan, 160
Aslib, *xii, xiii, xix*, 6, 33
Aspect systems, 74*ff*
Automation, *xv*, 84*ff*, 115*ff*, 151–2
  and abstracts, 103
  and classification, 44, 64
  commercial exploitation, 88
  and concepts, 64
  documentation, 19
  economics, 87
  and language, 144*ff*, 165*ff*

Automation (*contd.*):
  and librarianship, 123*ff*, 158*ff*
  psychology, 85
  and reference service, 158*ff*
  SDI, *xix*, 119
  and social data, 125
  technology, 89
  typesetting, 160
  WRU, 103*ff*

BACH, J. S., 93
Bacon, Francis, 56, 148
Barbier, A. A., 59
Barnard, Henry, 28
Batten system, 78
Bell Telephone Laboratories, 158
Belzer, Jack, 105
Bestermann, Theodore, 6, 23
Bibliofilm Service, 33
Bibliographic centers, 17, 34*ff*, 118,
  128
  see also Documentation
Bibliographic essay, *see* Literature
  surveys
Bibliographic Organization, 13, 18*ff*,
  22, 45, 132, 151
Bibliographic Society (U.S.), 34
Bibliographical Society (U.K.), 34
Bibliography, *xii*, 12, 33*ff*, 127
Binkley, Robert C., 109
Birmingham City Library, *xiv*
Bliss, H. E., 61*ff*, 141
Bohr, Niels, 136
Bonn, George S., 169
Booksellers, 42, 59
Boston, John of Bury, 23
Bouillaud, Ismael, 58
Bradford, S. C., *xiv*, 1, 21*ff*, 41
  Law of Scattering, 53
  and UDC, 43*ff*
Brain, pattern of operation, 64, 81–2,
  93, 142
Briet, Suzanne, 21, 72
British Association for the Advance-
  ment of Science, 30
British Museum, 35
British National Bibliography, xiv

British Society for International Bibliography, *xv*, 6, 33
Brown, James Duff, 60
Bruner, J. S., 67, 134
Brunet, J. C., 59
Bure, G. de, 59
Burnside, *General* Ambrose E., 91
Busa, *Father* Roberto, 79
Bush, Vannevar, 115, 118

CALLIMACHUS, 58
Camillo, Giulio, 58
Carnegie United Kingdom Trust, 6
Case Institute of Technology, 148, 152
Cassiodorus, 84
Catalogue of Scientific Papers, 3
Cataloguing and automation, 123, 160*ff*
    book form, 82, 84*ff*, 161
    books, 26
    co-operative, 46
    journals, 26
    multi-entry, 77
    origins, *xi*
    rules, 25
Categories, *xvii*, 60
    fundamental, 61, 65, 76
Center for Documentation and Communication Research, *see* Western Reserve University
Chaucer, Geoffrey, 91
Chemical Abstracts Service, 80, 108
Chicago, University of, 109
    Bibliographic Organization Conferences, 148
    Graduate Library School, 3, 85
    Library, 14
    students' grants, 173
Citation index, 160
Classification
    arrangement, 19, 128
    and automation, 128
    and bibliographic organization, 43
    books, 26, 57
    expansive, 59–60
    history of, 57*ff*
    journals, 26
    and language, 140
    linearity, 63
    origins, *xi*
    and retrieval, 74
    semantic factoring, *xvi*
    standardization, 52
Colon Classification, *xvii*, 44, 61, 76, 140
    see also Ranganathan, S. R.
Columbia University, 171
Colwell, E. C., 15
Comak, 79
Commerce Clearing House, 7

Communication, 65, 95, 135*ff*, 148, 154*ff*, 174*ff*
Computers, *see* Automation
Concepts
    formation, 64, 81, 154*ff*
    and language, 135
    in social science, 131
Concilium Bibliographicum, 4
Concordances, 160
Consensus, scientific and educational, 62
Consoles, 119
Content accessibility, 41
Co-ordinate indexing, 78
Cordonnier, Georges, 111
Council for the Study of Democratic Institutions, 159
Creativity, 65
Crestadoro, A., 160
Culture, 37
Current awareness service, *xivff*, *xviii*, 104, 151
Cutter, Charles Ammi, 25, 27, 59, 63, 77

DANA, John Cotton, 16, 33, 126
Data banks, 119, 126
Data processing, 118*ff*
    see also Automation
De Bury, Richard, 57
Decimal Classification
    Concilium Bibliographicum, 4
    first edition, 24–5
    rigidity, *xvii*
    teaching of, 49
    and UDC, *xv*, 4
    see also Dewey, Melvil
Democracy and education, 28, 30
Denison, Edward F., 157
Denudation, 61
Deposit libraries, *see* Storage libraries
Descriptive literature, 9
Descriptors, 79
Dewey, Melvil, 24, 35, 58*ff*, 75, 139
    see also Decimal Classification
Diebold, John, 161
Dissection, 61
Dissemination, *see* Information
Ditmas, E. M. R., 30
Document systems, 74*ff*
Documentary reproduction, 41, 46, 77, 118
Documentation
    and archives, 28
    centres, 17*ff*, 32, 118, 128
    definition, 3, 72
    and librarianship, 22*ff*, 68, 87
    personnel, 47
    profession of, 35, 48
    origin, 29

Documentation (*contd.*):
  secrecy, 88
  service, 16
  sources, 6
  users, 8
  see also Information
Doherty, Francis X., 15
Du Maine, Lacroix, 58-9
Duke University, 101
Dürer, Albrecht, 90

ECOLE des Chartes, 2
Edison, Thomas A., 67
Educators
  use of literature, 12
Edwards, Edward, *xi*, 27, 29
Egan, Margaret, 1, 21, 30, 52, 149, 175
Einstein, Albert, 66
Eliot, Charles W., 15
Eliot, T. S., *xix*, 70, 90
Ellison, *Rev.* John, 79
Engineering Societies Library, 7
Engineers
  use of literature, 147*ff*
English Teaching Abstracts, *xix*
Epistemology, 66
Erasmus, 54
Exchangeability in literature, 10

FACET analysis, *xvi*, 44, 49, 141
Facsimile transmission, 41
Fairthorne, R. A., 75, 105
Fano, R. M., 116, 158
Farradane, J. E., 44
Fédération Internationale de Documentation, 2
  foundation of, 5, 29
Fermi, Enrico, 106
Field, Herbert Haviland, 4
Film-O-Rex, 77, 111
Flett, L. H., 97
Flexner, Jennie, *xiv*
Flexowriter, 80, 100, 104
Focke, Helen, 102
Folger Library, 15
Fort Huachuca, Signal-Corps, 101
Foskett, D. J., 84, 177
Frank, Otto, 21
Freud, Sigmund, 66
Fussler, Herman H., 116
Fust, Johann, 58

GALEN, 23
Galileo Galilei, 56
Garfield, Eugene, 160
Gesner, Konrad, 23, 41, 58, 63
Giddings, F. H., 130
Gilbert, William, 57

Glass, Bentley, 150
Godet, Marcel, 5
Goodspeed, Edgar J., 109
Goethe, J. W. von, 137-8
'Graphic unit', 19, 23, 63
Gull, C. D., 164
Gulliver's Travels, 54, 68
Gutenberg, Johann, 56, 114, 175

HADLEY, Chalmers, 33
Hanson, C. W., *xiii, xiv*
Hanson, J. C. M., 60
Harris, W. T., 58
Harvard University, 15
Harvey, William, 57
Heisenberg, Werner, 136-7
Henkle, Herman H., 116, 169
Henry, Joseph, 30, 69
Herskowitz, Melville J., 135
Hertz, David, 154, 156
History of libraries, 55
History of scholarship, 55
Hook, Sydney, 92
Horne, T. H., 59
Humanists
  use of literature, 12
Huntington Library, 15

ILLINOIS Institutes of Technology, 158
Illinois, University of, 148
Index Bibliographicus, 5
Indexing
  co-operative, 26
Information
  BSIB, 33
  centres, 82
  classification, 34, 63
  coding, 142-3
  conceptual, 154-5
  dissemination, *xiii*, 32, 119
  empirical, 155
  procedural, 155
  retrieval, 63, 77*ff*, 90, 105, 143
  and scientists, 151*ff*
  in social science, 131
  stimulatory, 156
  training for, 169*ff*
  WRU, 80
  see also Current awareness service, Reference service, Retrospective searching
Instrumental literature, 10
Inter-library loan, 46
International Business Machines Co., Inc., 77, 111, 160
International Catalogue of Scientific Literature, 3, 30
International Committee on Intellectual Co-operation, 5

International Conference on Scientific Information, 1958, 148, 169
International Conference for Standards on a Common Language for Machine Searching and Translation, 1959, 141
International Federation for Documentation, *see* Fédération Internationale de Documentation
International Federation of Library Associations, 6
International Institute for Bibliography, 4
International Institute for Documentation, 4
International Institute for Intellectual Co-operation, 5
Intrex, 115*ff*
Isidore of Seville, 55

JEVONS, Stanley, 44
Jewett, Charles C., 6, 24, 27, 69
John Crerar Library, 15, 159
Jonker Business Machines Inc., 79
Journal of Documentation, 6

KENT, Allen, 102, 105, 134
Keppel, Frederick, 96, 112
Kern, Leo M., 1
Kessler, M. M., 116
Keyword-in-Context, *xvii*, 80, 160
Knowledge
   and automation, 123*ff*
   communication, 95
   Eliot, T. S., 70
   growth of, 70
   secrecy, 88
   systems, 73
   theory of, 66
   and wisdom, 70

LA Fontaine, Henri, *xiv*, 4, 22, 29, 35, 76
Lamination, 61
Lane, William Coolidge, 15
Langer, Suzanne, 65, 134
Language, 65, 74, 121, 126, 134*ff*, 165*ff*
League of Nations, 5, 47
'Library 21', 55, 162
Library of Congress
   Bibliographical Planning Group, 1
   cataloguing, *xiv*, 80
   classification, *xvii*
   mechanization, 80
   and research, 14
   searching, 92
   Union Catalog, 6
Library schools, *see* Schools of Librarianship

Licklider, J. C. R., 115–16
Literature surveys, *xx*, 13, 41, 155
Long Island Lighting Co., N.Y., 80
Loose assemblage, 61
Lotz, John, 136
Luhn, H. P., 80, 112

MABUN, Jean, 58
McCarthy, Stephen A., 116
McCulloch, Warren, 95
McGraw-Hill Publishing Co., 7
MAC-TIP Project, 116–17, 120
Mainz Psalter, 58
Mann, Horace, 28
Martel, Charles, 60
Martin, G., 59
Marx, Karl, 84
Mass media, 2
Massachusetts Institute of Technology
   Intrex, 115*ff*
   library, 14
   MAC, 158
Mazarin, Cardinal, 57
Mechanization, *see* Automation
Meier, R. L., 67
Melton, Jessica, 105
Melton, John L., 91
Mergenthaler, Ottmar, 114
Merlin, Romain, 58
Merton College, 56
Michael, Donald N., 159, 162
Microfilm, 112
Midwest Inter-Library Center, 15
Minicard, 77, 89, 111
Minnesota, University of, 54
Model library, 118*ff*
Modern Language Abstracts, *xix*
Mohrhardt, Foster E., 116
Molière, J. B. P. de, 141
Monasteries, 23
Mooers, Calvin, 79–80, 147
Morley, Linda, 102
Morris, Charles W., 135, 142
Morris, William, 84
Murphy, Gardner, 136
Murra, Kathrine, 1, 30

NATIONAL Academy of Sciences, 116, 169
National bibliography, 127
National Electronics Research Council, *xix*
National Science Foundation, 100, 169
Naudé, Gabriel, 57–8
Neumann, J. von, 64, 95
New England Deposit Library, 15
New York State Library, 79
Newberry Library, 15

Newton, *Sir* Isaac, 56
Nicolas of Cues, 56
Norwood, Sharon, 150

OPERATIONAL literature, 39
Oppenheimer, J. Robert, 70
Oresme, Nicole, 56
Otlet, Paul, *xiv*, 1, 4, 21–2, 29, 35, 76
Overhage, Carl J., 116–17
Overmeyer, LaVahn, 105

PALEOGRAPHY, 110
Palmer, B. I., 84
Panizzi, *Sir* Anthony, 27
Paris Booksellers, 59
Paris, University of, 56
Patent literature, 11
Peek-a-boo, 78, 110
Peloponnesian War, 90
Pergamum, 55, 71
Periodicals
  growth of, 25, 40
  indexing, 3, 25
  use of, 153
Perry, J. W., 91
Personnel, 47
Philosophy
  of librarianship, *xi–xii*, 37*ff*, 72*ff*,
    121, 126
Photon, 160
Physical accessibility, 40
Pickwick Papers, 78
Pierce, John R., 158
Poincaré, Henri, 65
Pollard, A. F. C., 33
Poole, W. F., 25, 27, 160
Pope Joan, 54
Popularization of science, 13, 57
Price, D. J. da S., 70
Printing
  computerized, 160
  invention of, 56, 114, 175
  new methods, 114
Public Libraries, 26
  Boston, 14
  Clerkenwell, 61
  Cleveland, 14
  King County, 79
  Los Angeles, 80
  New York, 14, 169
  popular reading rooms, 32
  and research, 14
  societies, 175
  subject departments, 32
Public Libraries Act, 1850, 29
Punched cards
  abstracts, 103
  edge-notched, 77, 110
  U.S. Patent Office, 80

Punched cards (*contd.*):
  WRU, 103
  see also Automation

QUADRIVIUM, 58

RANGANATHAN, S. R., *xvii*, 44, 61
  categories, 61, 65, 76
  facet analysis, 81
  reference service, 73
Rapid Selector, *xvi*, 77, 111
Recruitment, 169*ff*
Rees, Alan, 105
Reference service, *xii*, 31–2, 73, 90,
    120, 158*ff*
  see also Information
Reiser, Oliver L., 141
Remington-Rand Univac, 111
Renier, G. J., 131
Reports, 16, 31, 40
Research, 38, 52, 97, 108, 154*ff*
Research libraries, 14
Retrospective searching, *xiv*, 74
Rogers, Frank B., 78
Roget, Peter Mark, *xvi*
Rôle indicators, 81, 141
Rosenblatt, Frank, 159
Royal Society of London, 3, 30, 148
Rubenstein, Albert, 154, 156
Rules for a dictionary catalogue, 25

SAMAIN, Jacques, 77, 111
Sapir, Edward, 135
Savage, E. A., 32
Savage, L. J., 126
Sayers, W. C. Berwick, 44
Scattering, Law of, 53
Schoeffer, Peter, 58
Schools of Librarianship, 68*ff*, 169*ff*
  WRU, 99
Science Service, 33
Scientists
  and documentation, 86*ff*
  influence of, 57
  use of literature, 8*ff*, 87, 98, 148*ff*
Search strategy, 165*ff*
Selective Dissemination of Informa-
    tion, *xix*, 119
Semantic Code Index, *xvi*, 80
  see also Western Reserve University
Seven Liberal Arts, 58–9
Shackleton, Ernest, 90
Shannon, Claude, 95
Shaw, Ralph, *xvi*, 85, 111, 149
Sherrington, *Sir* Charles, 81, 95
Shores, Louis, 132
Simonton, Wesley, 54
Smithsonian Institution, 6, 24, 25,
    69

Snow, *Lord* (C. P.), 71
Social epistemology, 67, 154, 175
Social intelligence, 48
Social sciences, 42, 125
Social scientists
  use of data, 130
  use of literature, 12
Societies
  and communication, 67, 174*ff*
  growth of, 39
  professional, 42, 45, 177
  research on, 130
  technology, 39
Special libraries
  and dissemination, *xiiff*, 32
  documentation in, 7, 15
  research, 31
Special Libraries Association, 6, 33
Specialization
  for librarians, 49, 51
  in libraries, 32
Spenser, Edmund, 90
Sputnik, 171
Storage libraries, 15, 41, 83
Strauss, Lucille J., *xii*
Strieby, Irene, *xii*
Students
  use of literature, 12
Subject approach, *xiii*, 8*ff*, 29, 78
Subject bibliography, 23, 41, 49, 127, 161
Super-imposed coding, 77
Swift, Jonathan, 54
Swiss National Library, 5
Symbols, 141*ff*
  status, 175
  see also Language
Syntopicon, 55
Systems Development Corporation, 158

TAPE typewriters, 80, 158
Taube, Mortimer, 78
Technicians
  use of literature, 10*ff*
Technological literature, 38
Television, 119, 176
Telstar, 67, 158
Term entry systems, 78*ff*
Terminology, 74
  see also Language
Theophrastus, 55
Thesaurus, *xvi*
'Thought-unit', 19
Thurber, James, 72
Tolstoi, *Count* Leo, 96
Tomoski, Edward A., 97
Tornudd, Elin, 149
Trade bibliography, 24
Trade journals, 11

Training, 169*ff*
  see also Schools of Librarianship
Translation, 142–3
  mechanical, 101, 145
Tritheim, Johann, 23
Trivium, 58
Typesetting, 160

UNDERGRADUATE libraries, 31
UNESCO
  Bibliographical Planning Group, 1
  grants, 6
Union Catalogues, 24, 41, 69
United Nations, 47
U.S. Air Force, 100, 111
U.S. Army Medical Library, 7, 16
U.S. Bureau of the Census, 7, 160
U.S. Committee on Economic Development, 157
U.S. Department of Agriculture, 7, 16
U.S. National Aeronautics and Space Administration, 119
U.S. National Bureau of Standards, 160
U.S. National Library of Medicine, 7, 16, 78, 80, 119
U.S. Office of Censorship, 79
U.S. Office of Strategic Services, 79, 99, 112
U.S. Patent Office, 80
Uniterms, 78
Univac, 111
Universal Decimal Classification
  auxiliary signs, 76
  documentation, 44
  and language, 140
  origin, *xivff*, 4, 60
  teaching of, 49
  use of, 18
Universities
  libraries, 31
User Groups, *xix*

VENERABLE Bede, 23
Verhoeff, Jacobus, 105
Vickery, B. C., 44
Voigt, Melvin, 149, 151
Vormelker, Rose, 102

WALD, Abraham, 125
Walnut system, 77–8, 88
Walter, W. Grey, 95
Weinberg Committee, *xx*
Western Reserve University, *xvi*
  CDCR, 99*ff*
  coding, 141
  conferences, 148
  information retrieval, 80*ff*
  literature searching, 80, 112

Western Reserve University (*contd.*):
  staff, 105
  students' grants, 173
  User Groups, *xix*, 100
Westminster Gazette, 22
Whatmough, Joshura, 136
White, Stanford, 107
Whitehead, A. N., 44, 66
Whorf, Benjamin Lee, 136
Wiener, Norbert, 159, 163
William of Ockham, 55
Wilson, H. W., Co., 7

Winsor, Justin, 27
Wolfle, Dael, 97
Woodbine, Herbert, *xiv*
Woods Hole Conference, 1965, 116
Works Progress Administration, 17

YALE University, 25, 114
Yngve, Victor, 121
Young, Karl, 114

ZATOCODING, 79